SPIRIT
SPEAKS
WITHIN YOU

THE AWAKENING GUIDE TO TAP
INTUITION, GAIN VALIDATION
AND INCREASE HEALING

KELLE SUTLIFF

Praise for Spirit Speaks Within You

"Kelle has given us all the most wonderful gift. She has given every reader the tools to tune in and listen to our own guides, so that we may navigate life's challenges, and create the very best outcome for a rich and meaningful journey. I have been a client of Kelle's for many years. Her ability to hear and channel Spirit is a true blessing. Thank you, Kelle, for being so generous in sharing your intuitive knowledge so that each of us may learn how to listen to Spirit."

—Jani Guest, Creators, Inc. CEO

"Down to earth and spiritually informative! Kelle's spiritual experience & knowledge shines through in this easy read, direct and to the point, book. You will not want to put it down."

—Emilia Kelly, International Clairvoyant Consultant, Buckinghamshire, UK

"This latest release by Kelle is not only uplifting and inspirational but life-changing! She teaches the reader how to tap into their 'own' soul by listening to their clear intuition. *Spirit Speaks Within You* encourages you to follow your heart, enabling you to be open to the messages sent by your spirit guides. I've personally had several Readings by Kelle. They've each been spot on and accurate. More importantly, she's taught me how to trust in my divine and spiritual compass."

—D.D. Marx, International Best-Selling Author of *The Beyond Series*

SPIRIT SPEAKS WITHIN YOU

*The Awakening Guide
to Tap Intuition,
Gain Validation
and Increase Healing*

Kelle Sutliff

GLOBAL WELLNESS MEDIA
STRATEGIC EDGE INNOVATIONS PUBLISHING
LOS ANGELES, TORONTO, MONTREAL

First Edition. Published by:
Global Wellness Media
Strategic Edge Innovations Publishing
340 S Lemon Ave #2027
Walnut, California 91789-2706
(866) 467-9090
StrategicEdgeInnovations.com

Publisher's Note: The views expressed in this work are solely those of the authors and do not necessarily reflect the views of the publisher, and the publisher hereby disclaims any responsibilities for them.

Editors: Sarah Aschenbach, Shannon O'Keeffe Circelli
Book Design: Global Wellness Media
Cover Design: Shena Honey L. Pulido

Spirit Speaks Within You / Kelle Sutliff. -- 1st ed.
ISBN: 978-1-957343-02-0 (Kindle)
ISBN: 978-1-957343-03-7 (Paperback)

Disclaimer

The author is providing this book and its contents on an "as is" basis and makes no representations or warranties of any kind with respect to this book or its contents. The author disclaims all such representations and warranties, including but not limited to warranties of healthcare for a particular purpose. In addition, the author assumes no responsibility for errors, inaccuracies, omissions, or any other inconsistencies herein. The purpose of this book is to educate. It is not a replacement for medical advice.

Table of Content

Dedication

As many of us know and can feel, humanity—individually I dedicate this book to my dear mother, Marilyn "Mimi" Teets, and to my beloved friend, Clairvoyant Medium Bridget Benson, two soul sisters who passed away in 2020.

Bridget Benson wrote this poem and sent it to me when my mother died. I share it here for all of you who have experienced loss of a loved one.

"I thought about you, yesterday
But that was nothing new
I thought of you the day before
And the day before that, too
Whenever you need me
I will be there
And always remember you
In my prayer."

—Bridget Benson

Acknowledgments

These past few years, everyone in our world, including me, has been on a rollercoaster of emotions. Two of my best friends passed away in 2020, my mother in June and my friend Bridget in November—both of natural causes. Like many people dealing with loss, I felt that the rug had been pulled out from underneath me. That was when I decided to help people reconnect to their own Spirit guides, and this small book with a powerful punch was born. *Spirit Speaks Within You* is meant to realign your soul a bit, so you can trust again and connect to Spirit in so many ways.

When we have trauma or loss, we need to heal. This book will help you to do that. It will help you to break free from old patterns so that new experiences can begin to shift you and enhance the strength of your own soul.

I want to thank my family: my husband, Tom; my son, Matthew; and my Irish twin daughters, Avery and Haley. We have all learned a lot and grown during these past years, and to our credit. We did it without fear. We all get the star!

To my coaches who helped me birth this book, Shannon O'Keeffe Circelli, my marketing guru; Eric D. Groleau of Global Wellness Media; Sarah Aschenbach, my editor; and Shena Honey L. Pulido for my stunning book cover design.

A thousand thanks for your great knowledge and passion for this project.

Finally, I must salute the collaboration I received from my guides, passed loved ones, and that other team I reference throughout this book. You inspired me to write and bring the Divine into the hands of these readers. Thank you.

Big hugs all around,

Kelle

Introduction

This book is all about Spirit and your world and how the Divine is *in* you every single day, in every moment, until the end of your time here on earth. You were born naturally intuitive and with access to magical knowledge that creates in you an all-natural *flow*. It is no different from how your legs walk or your lungs breathe. Your Spirit (intuition) is your gift. It is natural. The Three Wise Men gave this to you when you were born. It's what I like to call the holy trinity of psychic ability. Why? Because when you work with divine information, you are your own conduit. It is that simple. It is one of the most powerful pieces of you; it defines your soul's need. It is part of your DNA.

In Matthew 2:1-12, wise men came to the East to visit Jesus, bearing gifts of gold, frankincense, and myrrh. This was the infant sent by God who was going to change the world, and the gifts were anointing oils that were rare and precious at that time: frankincense for anointing one's self in life; myrrh for anointing the dead (an unusual oil to give a baby, but they knew his future); and gold, an uncommon gift in those economic times.

What many fail to remember is that the three wise men, who were called "Magi," were highly regarded astrologers! They followed a bright star in the sky that led them to

Bethlehem. One was Persian, one Indian, and one Arabian, and they were highly respected for their inner gifts. So, there you have it: Jesus was blessed by *three astrologers* bearing beautiful gifts!

You, too, have been blessed. You were given a form of guidance, just as the Magi were guided to follow a particular star that night. They followed the bright star in the sky for days. They had no fear. They trusted their "inner knowing," which told them the journey had a purpose. You were blessed with that same amazing instinct. Spirit speaks within you to guide you during your life hierarchy.

One of the greatest revelations I have received as a psychic medium is that God talks to us through our psychic connection. There, I said it. Much of the religious upper echelon doesn't want you to believe this is true, but I am telling you that it is true. After eighteen years of doing countless psychic readings and hours upon hours of meditation, I can attest that God's energy comes through the psychic connection, and it is available to us all. Manmade laws often chastise such knowing influence, but I am here to tell you that God's psychic environment is very different. It is energy that comes from a deity of love, and you can connect to it through your own psychic gifts, which can be developed. Yes, Spirit really does speak within you.

As is stated in Joel 2:28 in The New International Bible, "It will come after this. I will pour out my Spirit on all of mankind. And your sons and daughters will prophesy, your old men will dream dreams, and your young men will see visions."

And in: John 1417: "The Spirit of truth. The world cannot accept him, because it neither sees him nor knows him. But you know him, for he lives within you and will be in you."

Now, those are some powerful words, don't you think? I am not a priest, rabbi, minister, or nun (although I did do twelve years of Catholic school, and that should count for something!) As a psychic medium, I am a daily reflection of information I receive from the higher realm. I see Spirit, some call it Holy Spirit, some call it the Divine, some call it God's presence. I know now that the energy is all the same, no matter how you label it.

It is most important to accept your intuition when you feel it speaking to you—or sometimes shouting at you. The source of that intuition is the presence of your Divine, whether it's God, Allah, Buddha, Grandma, or Dad, raising its vibration to give you a message. Why buck the system? It is about time we accept the source of psychic connection. It is that simple because it *is* simple.

Now that we are dealing with a worldwide pandemic and world conditions that shock us every day, don't you think it is time to stop fighting our intuition? Spirit is just plain part of us. It is our *flow*. It is our *vibe,* and it has been given to us in trust through an agreement with our souls that we accepted when we came to this earth. It is our own intuitive Holy Spirit. For example, try saying affirmations like, "For the highest and best good, I am listening to my instinct every day. I trust what Spirit gives me in guidance," and watch how Spirit captures your energy. I promise that you will see magnificent results. Who doesn't need real guidance these days? We all do! Your intuition will catch fire, your decisions will be on point, and your Spirit guides will applaud you!

"For the highest and best good, I am listening to my instinct every day. I trust what Spirit gives me in guidance."

The world situation today has forced us to question the meaning of life and cope with the reality of death. You may notice that you are more aware of what is around you, perhaps more aware of your inner state. The dangers today and the horror and the isolation have made many people more aware of their hunches and instincts. It has upped our psychic ability, and this ability will only continue to develop as we go on. Your number-one objective should be to listen to and trust the promptings of that psychic self of yours. So, stop delaying all the good outcomes you could be having, and please don't wait for the next pandemic to make you enlightened. Aren't we all kind of past this, by now?

We are lucky to have this intuitive vibration within us to help us synchronize with life. We have our own "psychic internet." All we have to do is flip it on to receive guidance. It's like holding the remote control to the television, and we all know there is a kind of power in that! Spirit is here to remind you that it is okay to reclaim and take control of your intuitive power.

Your Psychic Instinct

"And I will ask the Father, and he will give you another advocate to help you and be with you forever."
—John: 14:16

I interpret the word *advocate* in the above passage to mean your psychic instinct. Your advocate is your psychic internet. It is that hunch to try something new, to do something for your "greater good." And sometimes the hunch is to *refrain from* doing something for your greater good. Like a prophet, you foresee a good outcome. Yes, your psychic guidance is your prophet. You can be that powerful. Some of you simply accept this instinct, and some of you fear it. There is no reason to fear psychic ability when we now have so much more general awareness and experience on the subject. I am here to tell you it was given to you as a form of protection.

If you have faith in any kind of spirituality or religion, you know that fear keeps you stagnant. It keeps you from freeing your conscious mind. Spirit wants to assure those of you who are afraid that it is perfectly okay to be open to new ideas and experiences. As you consider the source of any fear you may have, here are a few questions to consider:

- **What circumstance closed you off from your intuitive *flow*?**
- **As a young child, were you told that your intuitive knowing was evil?**
- **Did you have experiences that made you scared?**
- **Did you have a trauma or loss when you expected your intuition to be there, and it wasn't?**
- **Why did you let this happen when Spirit guidance was with you every step of the way?**

As you ponder these questions, my guides hope you will realize that it is safe now to reopen your heart to your innate spirituality.

My guides and I hope that you will take that single step, that you will choose to trust the integrity of your psychic instinct, since this aspect exists in all of us. It is right there in you. You were born with it, and God gave it to you as a benefit, so don't stifle it. Just crack that little door open a tad wee bit and watch how the intuitive eternal sunshine fills your insight. Your guides will be so happy. "Yay, she's back!" or "Boy, where have you been?" they will exclaim.

It is certainly not complicated. Just listen within. I am here to remind you that *all* you have to do is crack that door a smidgen, open your mind, and revive your natural, God-given *flow* of intuition. Now, who is willing?

Your psychic ability comes from what I refer to as God's gut instinct. Now, that may sound odd to some, but the truth is that God's instinct is your instinct. Think about that statement for a minute:

God's instinct = Your instinct

If you believe in the power of God and nature and in the power of love and guidance, why shouldn't you believe that Spirit is in your own consciousness? You can and you should. It is time to advocate for yourself. Don't let anyone sway you away from your psychic instincts and the value of what it tells you. It is time to manifest your intentions and feel the glory of psychic ability, and there is no shame in that.

Wake Up

"Consciousness is the state of quality of awareness or being aware of an external object or something within oneself."
—Webster's Dictionary

Humans have the capacity to *feel* and to *be awakened*. As we feel our senses and become aware, our consciousness expands. It's how what I call our psychic internet evolves. The mind, body, and soul connect to make that happen. In my world, I cast a pretty wide "net," but I do this work for a living. I have to use all my senses to read for a client. I feel, hear, and see my clients' energy. To give out the information that's needed, I blend with it. As I am doing this, I know it is God's work, not mine. There should be no ego involved when you channel for someone or yourself.

How could I read for clients or help solve a missing persons case if my work was not supported by the divinity of Love? And that elephant in the room? That would be God. There, the secret is out. The reel of information flows from the Infinite, the Divine. I am here to tell you that Spirit is, by the Grace of God, right inside you. It has been there all this time, and you are to doubt this connection no more!

9

I remind you to trust because too many people have forgotten how to trust in themselves. People like to be guided by others. It's the easy way out. Nope! It's time to stand on your own two feet, grounded, and act on your own. Right now. Pretend I am your psychic Fairy Godmother and I am kicking your arse out of the nest right this instant! It's time to get busy. As Tom Brady (The GOAT), quarterback of the Tampa Bay Buccaneers, would say, "Let's Goooooo!" I like to think that is what your loved ones from the other side say when your soul contract is complete. They encourage you to leave this earth to come with them: "Let's Goooooo!" And you go and your team of loved ones embrace you. That is a pretty great ending to the game.

Today, I admire everyone's heightened consciousness as God's instinct talks through them. Whoa! Now that is a big statement I just made—that we are Godlike. You are Godlike. Maybe not so much when you were three years old or the wild teenager who was always right. But today, you have grown into your "God-hip-like presence" with your divine intuition. We were all born with this knowledge; it is making that beautiful choice to use it. Glory be! I say, mission accomplished.

Your intuition is always *one* with you. It speaks to you, but are you listening? Some days your psychic net may pick up a quiet whisper of your mind, like a "feeling" that something momentous is on the way, or an uneasiness that something is not quite right, or a sense that you've met someone who will be important in your life. Knowledge or messages may come through the body, such as an instinct to move one way or another when you are playing sports or to look in a certain direction to notice something important.

Sometimes our psychic net sends a danger alert. Most people blow this off. Animals don't. They couldn't survive if they did not listen to intuition. If God gave this instinct to animals to protect them, why would he *not* give humans the same instincts? Well, guess what? God did give it to us. Psychic ability is as natural as it gets, and we can believe in it. That is why our pet animals understand us. They use their sixth sense to read us daily. Maybe we need to be more like Rover, who can read the room more accurately!

"I remind myself every morning: Nothing I say this day will teach me anything. So, if I'm going to learn. I must do it by listening."
—Larry King, talk show host

We are using the internet, that worldwide web, *all* the time, but it is the wrong "net" to use 24/7 according to Spirit. God wants you to use a different kind of internet, the beautiful psychic net of inner knowing, just like animals do, by listening to and trusting what they *know* all the time. Google is not their friend. Intuition is their friend, just as it should be for you. Animals look at things with some caution. They question, and they listen. When they hunt for food, they never give up because their intuition never stops. They don't let fear or failed attempts deter them. They don't become passive victims. And we humans need to take that ugly word *victim* out of our personal vocabulary and continue our "hunt" by relying on instinct. Now, that is real power.

Listening is one of the most important components of psychic ability. Did you listen to your instincts in 2020 as the pandemic came on, and now in 2021 as it has persisted, and as you contemplate your future in 2022 and beyond? I bet you did, and you do. One good thing that has occurred from this pandemic is that many of us discovered our psychic abilities as we tried to survive! I have been waiting for this moment for a very, very long time. Society is awakening, and this is fantastic news.

The people I work with in readings understand that coincidences are real. People trust their inner voice about what to change or not to change in their life path. They seek the quiet in meditation, prayer, or some form of solitude so that they can be present as they make decisions and receive psychic advice. The Universal energy is increasing as people raise their individual vibration. This has been happening for many years now, which is lovely. Society has finally chosen to get out of the low consciousness vibration of chaos and take on this new opportunity as one. Hooray! Our world is understanding that psychic intuition rocks!

"Knowing" things is your strength. Remember that. Believe in your instinctual knowing. Try to believe that your intuition and natural instincts are there to protect everything in your life! Why would Spirit *not* give you such strength?

*"Your psychic flow functions naturally, just
like the circulatory system in your body."*

You are not conscious of your heart beating, right now. It just does. Your psychic *flow* is similar. God's energy provides your psychic *flow* to help you learn to trust yourself. It's a beautiful thing, this thing called *Flow*. It is the beating heart of connection, and it vibrates with the answers you seek. It is simply the intuitive soul that you naturally are. You have the God-given ability to be a psychic superhero. For myself, I am envisioning Wonder Woman but with smaller boobs? You?

Flow

*"Those who flow as life flows know
they need no other force."*
—Lao Tzu

I have now captured you with a lot of love and you are mine for the next few minutes. Here is a visualization demonstration on how to obtain your flow daily. Now, please follow my lead.

- Close your eyes.
- Visualize that God is handing you a flower, right now.
- Take a moment and visualize a pretty flower, its petals, its color, its fragrance.
- Now think of the word *flower*. What word does *flower* have in it? It's the word *flow*.
- Let your mind visualize this flower and think on how perfect it is, just like you.
- Say, to yourself how wonderful you are just like when you admire a beautiful bloom.
- You are presently in your natural flow.
- Now open your eyes, take a breath, exhale and enjoy your new peace.

If the seed of that flower (mine was a rose) is not planted in the soil of Mother Earth, it can't develop a root and bloom, it won't come alive and share its beauty. Just like that, your energy is like a flower. I'm a rose, you are a rose, and God is a big bouquet, ready to hand one right back at you—but *only* when you manifest your *flow*. That is a pretty cool analogy, and pretty simple. How big is your bouquet these days? My bouquet is the one with the extra blooms, one of those superior bouquets with bigger flowers you spend an extra ten dollars for. Don't think cheap. Think superior.

Back at Christ Good Shepherd School in Lincoln Park, Michigan, my teacher, Mrs. Poloit, gave us our first seed to plant in dirt in a Dixie Cup. We put those seed cups on the windowsill to mature and watered them every day. Every kid has done that experiment in school. I know you did it too. As that young kid, you probably didn't doubt that your seed would grow into a beautiful flower, right? You imagined a major bloom happening, and then it did! You trusted in the experiment. You didn't know how it was going to happen, but you still trusted in nature.

Even when "the smart girl" in the class thought she had bragging rights (ego) on how tall her flower grew, Mrs. P (God) put that chick right back in her place and the whole class, I remember, secretly loved it. That lesson was called you reap what you sow.

Life is the same way. You reap what you sow. But when any conflict messes with your *flow*, you can always make a choice to align yourself again. Remember that.

As little kids, there was no question that we would trust the unknown. Now that you are all "adulting," your life experiences are teaching you to trust your psychic intuition. Sometimes, unfortunate circumstances get in the way of our natural *flow*, and sometimes we really stink at trusting our instincts. Those are the moments we need to trust our intuition the most.

As we have learned from the pandemic, life can be hard and can even seem out of control. Gradually, but through adversity we mature in our intuition. Psychic ability has many stages, like the stages in the development of a flower. Growing your intuition is natural. Once you decide to throw a little fertilizer on your process, just watch how you will flourish! Before you know it, your garden will be full of tall, stunning roses, and not the cheap ones. Superior roses!

Just as we trust that a flower will grow from a seed, we can trust the *flow* of our instinct to help us survive and thrive. Trust, and you will bloom into the prettiest flower ever. Without trust, we are just weeds that get torn out of the garden. Remember, your goal is to be a rose, not a weed! Sink roots into your instincts, trust your process, and before you know it, you'll be the best dang flower in that garden. You may never look at a flower the same way again. In my world, the flower is the best visual my guides have given me in a long time, that and Mrs. Poloit at age six.

Let's talk about *Flow*…

I like to look at the word *flow* as:

F	**Follow**
L	**Love**
O	**Outwardly accept**
W	**Win**

That is *flow* in a nutshell. It cannot be accomplished without your psychic trust that Spirit is within you. Botch up those letters and you don't get the Win. Often, we get hard lessons, and we absolutely hate it when that happens. We have all been there, especially nowadays. We have seen lots of world challenges, government challenges, work challenges, children challenges, health challenges and, unfortunately for some, death. This is not just because of a pandemic! Many, many souls were ready to transition in that year of 2020. We didn't need a pandemic for their souls to leave; that would have happened anyway because their "soul time" on this earth plane had been completed.

When our soul pattern has connected that last dot, it enters the next dimension into God's pure love. We see an ending in death, but it is not an ending. For the soul, death is just the beginning of aliveness. Pandemic or no pandemic, when our journey is complete, we all move on to greater glory.

> *"What was once enjoyed and deeply*
> *loved, we can never lose, for all that we*
> *love deeply becomes part of us."*
> —Helen Keller

I believe that the deaths occurring in the pandemic are similar to the fate of 9/11 souls. They all were meant to leave at the same time. People dying today are a collective, and they all flow right into Spirit together, just like on September 11, 2001. That event taught the world many lessons. It was a true conflict of Good vs. Evil. We all felt it and experienced it. This pandemic is no different. Energetically, it is teaching us the same thing again.

We have seen the good and evil in all people's actions throughout this past year. Through our instinct, we are being shown how we *must* love with contrite hearts and humble ourselves to become better human beings, living without evil. But most important, we must trust the Spirit within us to know what evil is, and then listen so that Spirit can guide you.

It has been tough for everyone. We have had to learn to stay out of the weeds and try to flourish into beautiful roses while dealing with extremely difficult life lessons. We have had to figure out how to stabilize our future, remembering that the *constitution of ourselves* is the most important. We've had to flow so much, we didn't even know we were doing it. Did any of you feel like a salmon struggling to lay eggs, swimming upstream, pushing against a vicious current? I'll bet you did. The whole darn world did.

When you start to understand why we are here, that we were granted the gift of *flow* in our lives, you will understand exactly why Spirit gave it to us. Faith reminds us, or should remind us, of this daily. Usually, when we are *out* of *flow*, we want to run back to that other four-letter word that rhymes with *truck*, and you all know *exactly* what that is!

You may have uttered several *trucks* recently, or even just yesterday! And understand that, in that moment, you literally created chaos because you did not stay in *flow*. Remember to apply the words:

F	**Follow**
L	**Love**
O	**Outwardly accept**
W	**Win**

Follow, love, outwardly accept, and win to all your situations and watch how your instinct guides you. You will be amazed in your transformation.

Now it is time to put away the *trucks*, the chaos, and get everything back into order, into your *flow*. You may think that 2020 and 2021 have taught you enough, but have they?

"Your mind is a garden. Your thoughts are the seeds. You can grow flowers or you can grow weeds."
—Author Unknown

2021 and 2022

"Now is the time to do you."

This is a different calling. All of your intuition must be on high alert to create your highest and best intentions. 2021 and 2022 are smarter years. They signify freedom and liberty all across the world. I know that does not seem possible with the fighting in the Middle East and the chaos happening within world governments and even in our own countries or local communities. Chaos has stuck its ugly head into every level of society. Honestly, can we humans take on anymore? We sure can. We have the energy of the pioneers, and no wolf will harm your family or your land while you are on watch.

Freedom and liberty always begin with you first, and nothing else, not a government and not a country. You obtain them through your goals and your guidance for your own life. You must expect freedom and liberty and accept them into your soul in order to foster them in the world. It is time to move on and let go of the emotionality and misinformation 2020 brought. 2021 and 2022 are all about liberty and freedom. You need to say goodbye to the heartache of delusional impressions so that your liberty and freedom can begin—yesterday! I know you can make this transition. Just trust Spirit in you. There is such merit to who you are. It is time to start using it for your highest and best good.

I have a beautiful friend named Sally Silver. She is about as salt of the earth as a psychic medium can get. We often talk about destiny, I'd like to share her take on it, which I find interesting and valid:

> *"Destiny is like a stamp on your soul it propels you into the direction of the divinely ordained. We design firsthand our life path which is designed in our birth chart. You pick your soul lessons. How adversity is handled is all perception. When you have spiritual challenges, it is an opportunity for you to grow. It is how you work through it is the real challenge. The more growth we have the more evolution of life we obtain and become Spiritual human beings.*
>
> *This should be our main focus of our life. There is too much focus on the material world. It is the Spiritual piece that matters most. This is why so many people are not centered on their true destiny. It is so simple sometimes we just miss it."*
> —Rev. Sally Silver, Spiritualist

When you can align yourself with your true path, freedom, liberty, and destiny, the highest vibration occurs within your soul growth. We all have grown during the past few years, have we not?

> *"I believe the Holy Spirit exists in everyone."*
> —Rev. Sally Silver, Spiritualist

If we do not have soul growth, we do not have liberty and freedom. It truly comes down to our choices and our destiny. It has been hard for all of us. We had to rest and retreat a little to understand the dynamics of what was happening. Many of us had to go into quiet contemplation to figure out our lives. Now that you have done some research and have some answers, it is time to make a wish for manifesting your liberty and freedom. Empowerment will be amazing. This is what the world crisis should have taught you.

Always Look Backward to Go Forward

"You can't connect the dots looking forward; you can only connect them looking backwards."
—Steve Jobs

Most people dislike being out of *flow* with Spirit. It is chaotic. We have all been burnt by not listening to our intuition. Boy, can we tell stories about our past lessons!

When I read for clients, Spirit always makes me "look backward to go forward" to help them make sense of the information guides and loved ones are giving. They want us to see our patterns. In other words, our guides are keeping score! Tough events happen to all of us, but how much do you actually remember them and learn from them? Do you just keep repeating the same old lessons? The more you repeat, the harder it gets, and Spirit has a hard-right hook, remember that! You want to learn from your lessons on the first go-round, not the third, as each time you don't act appropriately, your experience is harsher.

Here is a personal example from my life. It's an oldie, but a goodie. I am sharing this story with you as never told before, because I feel it has an excellent message on what happens when you don't trust your instinct. So here we go, looking backward to go forward.

In 2006, my children were wee ones, ages five, six, and eight. We decided to move from the South Shore to the North Shore of Boston to shorten my husband's commute, which was well over two hours each way. Now, if you live in Boston, that means crossing the mighty Zakim Bridge ("The Lenny,") which is a huge deal if you live on the other shore of the city. Boston folk just don't do that! You always stay on the shore you grew up on! So, it was a difficult decision, but the right one. And so, we embarked on the arduous process of a move.

The For-Sale sign went up. I am a realtor and list my house with my firm. At that time, I was still a closeted psychic medium. I had simply *not* come out of my safe closet to tell everyone what kind of agent I *really* was— you know, the agent who represents dead people, the one who knows things before they happen—that kind! As typical in the real estate market, I got two offers right out of the gate. We took the highest offer, like everyone does, not the logical one, which included a hundred-thousand-dollar deposit.

Spirit told me to take another direction with the offers being presented, but I was not listening to my *flow*. I was all about the money, like everyone is when it comes to business. Well, that choice would later throw our world out of *flow*. Our choice of buyers bred chaos in the months ahead. *Trucks, trucks* and even more *trucks* riddled my year, just like 2020 did for us all.

Our logical Offer B walked away, and sparkling Offer A says all is fantastic until two days before our closing when a real estate field card mistakenly identified my house as a different style, which played with the value placed on the home. The buyer's appraisal therefore came in low to reflect comps of a multi-level home. Mind you, the buyers had been in my home four times to see what they were purchasing. I had two floors above the basement, so legally it was a colonial. Once I discovered the field card issue, I addressed it at Town Hall, with attorneys and real estate agents involved. It should have been no big deal, right? Nope, the stress began and here came the *trucks*!

Our life flipped on a dime on the day of our closing appointment when our buyers didn't show up! My house contents were on trucks, my Mom and Dad had arrived from Michigan to help us move, and we had two hours to get a bridge loan on our new property, so we wouldn't lose our deposit! We were easily in the heart-attack zone. I am shocked no one had one. Where was the bouquet of roses that should have been mine?

We had to carry a double mortgage payment until we could sell our old house. During that time, the market dipped, and our house stayed on the market for six months. Lots of bad words were said and tears shed in those months, and behind those words were prayers! But it wasn't over yet. Boom! The sparkling would-be buyers sued us and everyone who had touched their loan. Yes, I, too, was included in their plans for money.

My beautiful move across the Zakim Bridge in Boston turned out to be a living hell of lawsuits and lost income, tarnishing the beautiful energy of a new space to live in. My home was filled with anger. (*Truck! Truck! TRUCK!*) My husband was working ninety hours a week at a startup company, trying to get it off the ground. I had met no one in my new town, yet. I was traveling every weekend, crossing "The Lenny" to conduct open houses to sell this property.

The market knew I was desperate for a buyer. It was horrible. Finally, eleven months later, the court ruled in our favor, and we collected their deposit. Yes, the court decided that, indeed, the buyers had breached their contract with us. If only I had listened to the little voice that told me to take the other offer. But I got greedy. How often have you gotten greedy instead of listening to that little voice?

I thought I had survived the most stressful event in my life, but more was to follow.

I was in Michigan, visiting my folks with the kids. My Father had a bad cough. When I hugged him as he was dropping us off at the airport to return to Boston. I heard my guides say, "It's cancer in his lungs." Let me tell you, I hugged him extra hard that morning, but I said nothing to my father about what Spirit had told me. I did not want to believe what my intuition had just shared with me.

I was blocking my *flow*. This was my second lesson about not wanting to hear a forewarning from Spirit. How often do you blow off guidance off like I did? A few weeks later, my Dad would be diagnosed with stage 4 melanoma, and my world staggered from one hot mess to another, tugging on all my emotions.

I was living out of state with my terminally ill father, raising three little kids while my husband worked a million hours trying to get a company off the ground. I was in a new community where I still didn't know many people. I felt like I was drowning in quicksand.

I cried in the shower, I cried after parent drop-off, I pretended everything was fine as I drove the kids to practice, as I made dinner and threw my husband a hot plate at nine p.m. when he walked in the door. The year that I was forty was the most stressful of my life, both financially and emotionally of my life. And I was dealing with it all alone. Or so I thought.

In challenging times, I was never alone, and neither were you.

Later, I learned that I had not been alone in these catastrophes. My soul was moving toward a new job. I would have a new path, and I had to trust in my *flow* to survive it all. God was whispering to my psychic net all that year, showing me how to recognize that my gut instinct is God's instinct talking to me. You had better listen when your inner voice is whispering that, for example, you should take the stronger offer and not be greedy. That experience proved to me that life is easier when you stay in *flow* and listen to what your gut instinct is telling you, because it is *always* 100 percent correct!

God was whispering to my psychic net all that
year, showing me how to recognize that my
gut instinct is God's instinct talking to me.

My psychic net was screaming at me, but I chose not to listen. Have you been there? It's an ugly place, isn't it? The life example I just shared with you happened a long time ago, but it still feels like yesterday. You know you have grown because life/God taught you a lesson. I'm sure you all can remember a few lessons like that of your own. Can you remember what they have taught you? *Think hard and wisely and don't repeat them, learn from them.*

"Remember you cannot hold bliss in your fist.
You can hold bliss only in your open hand."
—Osho

Divine Order

"The spirit of love arranges all meetings in divine order for the highest good of all concerned."
—Alan Cohen

During that challenging year, I had to find a lot of love, which is hard to do when you feel that you are being attacked. I kept saying, "Everything happens for a reason," and it usually does. Life events always happen to correct themselves according to divine order, which is something all souls must agree to when they come into this world. Your soul signed on the dotted line to accept God's divine order, and sometimes that means it's not according to your own time frame. During that crazy year, I had to trust that to be true. And what other choice do you have when a tragedy strikes? You get humbled very quickly and accept events in divine time!

Inwardly, I had to accept the Outcome, the big *O* in the word *flow,* and know that, at the end of the tragedy, I would Win despite lawsuits, financial stress, marriage stress, and eventually the death of my dear dad. I had to learn a lot all at once while I was being taught to trust my psychic net to support me. I had to work hard to open myself to trust in the Divine and get into that *flow* I was so yearning for.

Think of a time in your life when certain choices threw your life into utter chaos. What would you have done differently? What did you learn from it? I know no one wants to go back to those moments, but as I say in my readings, Spirit always makes me look at your past to look into your present. In other words, *I have to look backward to go forward.* You know why? Because your past teaches you. It creates a divine order, just the response from God that you need.

> ### "If I understand change, I shall make
> ### no great mistake in Life."
> —Confucius

Take the risk

When you are not in *flow,* but you need to take the risk of accepting a new path, your God-given instinct tells you to trust. It's one of the hardest lessons you will ever be given. Just remember, you will never be alone. From that life experience in 2006, I discovered the knowledge of *flow*. Life gave me the obstacles so I could teach you what I learned today. Truly, I wish I had not been hit so hard, but it was part of the plan and part of my soul acceptance.

Today, I am thankful for the growth. When you are having such learning experiences, try to remember to be humble and thankful. Thank the experience. It is making your soul grow even more.

What happened to my world during that trying year of 2006? I no longer wanted to serve my community selling real estate, even though I had four offers from local agencies in my new town. I left six years of referrals from sellers on the table. I listened to my God-given instinct, said, "*Truck* it" and opened my practice as a psychic medium. My practice became a full-time career, radio opportunities came my way, and before you know it, I had my own weekly radio program, "Psychic Cup of Coffee," broadcast in four cities in the United States.

Soon, I kept hearing my instinct telling me to write, so I did. I was afforded the opportunity to contribute a chapter called "Daily Cup of Calm" to the book, *Pearls of Wisdom: 30 Inspirational Ideas to Live Your Best Life Now,*" with Jack Canfield and other New York Times bestselling authors. Then came the thought, "I have a few books in me," and I trusted that guidance, too. It took me down the publishing path to share my work with others. My first book, *Listen Up the Other Side IS Talking,* was born in 2014 and won two book publishing awards. Pinch me! In 2020, my work as a psychic medium and highly gifted intuitive was featured in *The Gift Within Us,* by Mary Ann Bohrer.

This *flow* of events is happening because I believe in my psychic net and my psychic future. After appearing on several radio and television interviews and multiple podcasts, I was rewarded by the opportunity to take on missing persons cases. "Oh, dear Lord, how can I do this?" I thought. "Now, you want me to find the missing?"

Many psychic mediums do not do this work because it is heavy and emotional. Trust me, I was intimidated, but since I got my first case twelve years ago, I have never looked back. (Thank you, Joann Matouk-Romain, for guiding me to help find your body.) A case that should have been solved, in my opinion, if the State of Michigan would have done a proper investigation. I have assisted in many cases (too many!) over the years. I have been successful in my psychic detective work. This adventure has been pretty amazing and shocking all at the same time. I have looked for people all over this planet, and that work continues today in my readings and case work.

My bouquet is looking pretty full! I love how *flow* works. And in this moment—I can't believe I am saying this—I am glad our house sale fell through. If it hadn't been for that awful situation, I would not be who I am today.

And similarly, through all of your own experiences, you have grown on your spiritual path. Remember, always, that you have to look backward to go forward to optimize your growth. Please don't forget all your negative experiences. Raise the bar and tell your children how they can overcome adversity. You need to show them your grit. Grit is a life force in all of us. Our history holds the key to all of our lives—the good, the bad, and even the ugly. Our history should always keep us humble.

> *"To improve is to change, so to be perfect*
> *is to have changed often."*
> —Winston Churchill

Change

We have to accept change in life and not fight it, always knowing that there is a better path for us. We all know that change kicks us out of our sandbox, and that can be hard, real hard. As a result of those changes, however, we may end up in a better sandbox with softer sand and a prettier pail and shovel—right?

2020 left no rock unturned for me or for any of us, but during that time, I kept in mind my trying year of 2006, and it guided me in maintaining my *flow*. Did you remember troublesome years of the past to get you through this crazy-making, unpredictable time? I will bet that you did, too.

Honestly, all I had to do was to say the number 2006 and see it in my mind's eye to keep myself grounded. I knew that Spirit was with me every step of the way. It was not easy when my lovely, ninety-one-year-old mother had a stroke in April and died of complications in June, during the pandemic. It was not easy losing my soul sister Bridget Benson, an amazing clairvoyant medium, five months later. During this pandemic, my grief has been huge, like my year 2006 on steroids. Let me share why.

I have traveled more than ever before in this short time. I was living in three states Michigan, Massachusetts, and North Carolina, dealing with different regulations everywhere I went. The matter of masking was always at the forefront. It took twenty-five open houses to sell our house in Massachusetts. We moved to North Carolina, and then there were four moves in four weeks as my kids moved to and from college and into new apartments. My family missed out on two college graduations, like so many families in the country. My son broke his ankle and six months later his elbow, both requiring surgeries. At the beginning of the pandemic, I picked up our daughter at the airport as she arrived home from college, and our sweet corgi, Mabel passed away on March 13th. "Welcome home, honey, now we have to put the dog down!" We thought our other dog needed a friend, so we added Millie, a Corgi puppy into our family, like many families during this pandemic. Yes, I was training a puppy during all of this turbulence. And I'd had the nerve to complain about 2006? There were so many endings and beginnings happening all at once that it was hard to find my joy, like so many of us that year.

Every month, there was something new to contend with, and there were no simple solutions. All were big life choices. It was dramatic. I cannot believe I am still standing. People everywhere became pioneer stock—whether we wanted to or not. Spirit wants to tell you that you were amazing, taking on challenges and listening to your guidance. Now, we all need to exhale. Give yourself a good pat on the back! You are a survivor. You contended with life's obstacles, with all of what 2020 dished out, and you empowered yourself to learn from all those situations.

During the trials of 2020, I constantly told myself, "If I was able to do 2006, I can do this. I am just going to stay in my *flow*, and Spirit please help me." I accepted the pandemic and the crazy flow of energy. I also accepted what was happening in my personal life. We all had to. The key word for 2020 was *acceptance*. We all had to accept change in some form, and if nothing else, we learned new ways to stay healthy. Holistically, our minds, bodies, and souls were in our hearts for the first time in a long time. People had empathy and love. Were you able to find love even in your grief? I know you did, because Spirit was wrapped all around you every step of the way.

Exhaling Fear

"For God has not given us a Spirit of fear, but of power and of love and of sound mind."
—2 Timothy 1:7

I accepted the results of my choices and my circumstances during 2020, and in the end, I got the *W* for *Win.* I won, I grew, and I changed because I did not give in to my fears. I put up a sign in my house: PLEASE *DO NOT FEED THE FEARS.* Did you feed your fears during 2020, and do you still feed into fears? Be honest with yourself. I could not have managed my 2020 if I'd allowed *any* fear to persist. If I had engaged in fear-based thoughts, I would have gone out for toilet paper and never come back! And I am not kidding.

Look at your 2020 story. How much did you trust your *flow* and your instinct? Did you feed into your fears? I know you felt afraid, and I know you grew. This whole darn world did! Looking back, how did you handle it? In other words, how was that *flow* treating you?

Remember, there is no fear in love, but there is punishment in fear itself.

In this exact moment, I want you to take a deep breath. A really soft breath. Let that softness fill your chest with love. As you breathe out, let go of any anxiety you still feel from 2020. All that heaviness will not serve you. Your breath is your miracle worker. It gives your body the kindness it needs. It feeds your intuitive mind to keep you in balance. It is time for you to breathe in your good and exercise the worthiness you deserve right now.

Let go of the chaos that 2020 brought into your world. It no longer defines you. Appreciate it, because it is a part of your history. You learned a great deal about humanity. Today, however, your job is to let what is old out so that what is new can come in. It is that simple.

Your lungs detoxify your whole body. Make a conscious effort to inhale and exhale deeply every day. Do it now. Breathe in and breathe out. You can will the body to clear itself. If you smoke, quit. If you vape, quit. You need these beautiful organs, and you must keep them clean. If we know anything after Covid-19 and Sars-2, we know how important it is to have healthy lungs. Your lungs and your immunity work together to raise your vibration so you won't get sick. They are a team of energy working every day for you. It's time to honor them.

Make a conscious effort to inhale and exhale deeply every day.

I know you have it in you to face your fears and accept change. 2020 and 2021 have taught us well. Spirit is like a home. It's a place you feel safe, loved, and respected. It is always with you, and it tries to spare you the heartache of life's choices. I purposely am not using the term *safe space,* because I believe it is a threatening term, and Spirit knows this, too! Please take that word out of your vocabulary. When we say, "safe space," our energy goes "on guard." We create a low consciousness by using certain words. Words send out energy that can defeat you because your words show you are willing to be defeated. Come on, you are better than that! You are a strong soul. Think like a rose, not like a dandelion. Remember, you are that superior bouquet we talked about earlier, and not the cheap one.

Society, You Are Healthy and Beloved

"Wherever a beautiful soul has been there is
a trail of beautiful memories."
—Ronald Reagan

We are so lucky that we have life to live and God's beautiful embraces to show us our intuition. You don't need scary words to define you. Who you are is not defined by a pronoun either. How about just being a soul? Now, there is a concept! We are here on this earth to do *really* good things, not sabotage it with crazy media words that make us feel less than whole. Everyone quit acting like the boogie man is coming to get you! Only you can come after you. Listen to Spirit within, and you will protect your energy like an armored tank. Harm? What harm? Don't even think about it. Do you see where I am going with this?

Speaking of tanks, can you imagine what all those World War II souls on the other side are saying about these times right now? They would say that terms like *safe space* or *my journey* are overused. They would tell us to just live life and make it work like they had to. Great advice. No one gave them a pass. They respected themselves enough to get themselves together and perform as humans are supposed to. They were a pretty simple generation. The only word like *journey* you are going to get out of those veterans is a song like "Sentimental Journey," a 1940s love song.

It's time to get real with Spirit; no more crutches or excuses and categorizing yourself or culture canceling. Life is what it is, and we have to learn from it and from our choices. There is nothing new about that. It's been this way for eternity and will continue. You are just a soul making choices in *flow,* and that's it! Please do yourself a favor: accept your role in your soul path, make good choices, and stop complicating what you yearn for. Make your "yearny" part of your journey.

The song "Sentimental Journey" has a great message. Read on...

Gonna take a sentimental journey
Gonna set my heart at ease
Gonna make a sentimental journey
To renew old memories

Got my bag, got my reservation
Spent each dime I could afford
Like a child in wild anticipation
I long to hear that 'All aboard!'

Seven, that's the time we leave, at seven
I'll be waitin' up for heaven
Countin' every mile of railroad track
That takes me back

Never thought my heart could be so yearny
Why did I decide to roam?
I gotta take this sentimental journey
Sentimental journey home

Seven, that's the time we leave, at seven
I'll be waitin' up for heaven
Countin' every mile of railroad track
That takes me back

Never thought my heart could be so yearny
Why did I decide to roam?
I gotta take this sentimental journey
Sentimental journey home

—Lyrics from *Sentimental Journey* by
Les Brown and Ben Homer

How do I know this song? Here is a fun memory: My father's family hosted a birthday party every year for my grandmother, Mae Teets, who lived to the ripe old age of ninety-seven. The "orchestra" as my grandmother called it, which was actually my cousins' garage band, played at every party. They'd hand over their mics yearly for my mother and five aunts. "Sentimental Journey" was their jam! My grandmother had a great big smile on her face as they all sang yearly. The crowd just roared!

It was not until I was older that I understood the meaning in those lyrics. You need to find what your heart yearns for and know that your "yearny" is a part of your soul path. Listen to your intuition and imagine where those train tracks of life can take you. Instead of allowing fear into your life, be excited about it. That is how Spirit understands those verses also.

2020 and 2021 have taken us into uncharted territory. We all toasted the 2020 New Year, thinking we were on that railroad track with new goals and calculating how we will move successfully into that new year goodness—then Boom! The pandemic, Covid-19/Sars-2, lockdowns, no toilet paper, and even death for many. It has turned into a total crap show, throwing too many people into fear, financial ruin, grief, anxiety, mental illness, and frustration about our future, not to mention political unrest and lack of trust in government leadership for some.

This has been a reset. The situation has changed the world, no matter what side you are on. The only reset you need is to remember that you are on God's team. When you work from a place of faith, you are empowered to kick ass and take names. Your soul, your intuition, and the Spirit of enlightenment fill you with joy, training your mind to be happy, even in unrest and chaos. If you think like this, you will always be able to put fear aside.

"There are two ways of spreading light: to be the candle or the mirror that reflects it."
—Edith Wharton

Lessons

"If you want to find the secrets of the universe,
think in terms of energy, frequency and vibration."
—Nikola Tesla

What lessons we have learned these past two years! Some lessons were for the better and some for the worse. Your soul has grown just as mine has during my ordeals in 2006 and then in 2020. So many empathic experiences were there for everyone. We all grew in empathy. Darn, the energetic lessons of the pandemic have been so difficult and full of misinformation. I felt it in *all* the readings I did for clients who lost loved ones due to complications from Covid-19/Sars-2. I have to be honest that in all my work during this time, I have done only nine readings of souls who died from Sars-2 complications, and I read daily for clients. You would think that a medium would have been inundated with such readings, but I wasn't. That's because the loss of jobs, the strain (or worse) on relationships, and children not being educated properly was over the darn top in the destructive department. It makes you question how things could have been handled differently and why they weren't.

We have also seen political chaos in our elections, and not just here in the US, but all around the world. These situations have been a total smack down of society. It has created a lot of anger and conflicting agendas among the media. This has gone far beyond what we are used to. Where is Walter Cronkite when we need him? "Calling in all Walters! Can you just report the facts and nothing but the facts and stop your sensationalism?" The media is like that person everyone dislikes but puts up with. All that person does is talk about themselves 24/7, and half the crap they say is nonsense? This is the media today. It's all about different agendas and not at all what Walter Cronkite would do. Unfortunately, we have endured constant chaos and pandemonium with people in the press pointing of fingers every which way. Sadly, too many humans have gotten caught up in the frenzy of some very strange agendas. Spirit was like, "What the *truck*?"

Our society has experienced censorship. You can consider yourself lucky if you were *not* thrown into social media jail for expressing your First Amendment rights, right here in the United States, and anywhere in the world that used to value free speech. I am letting you know that God did give you a soul that has an opinion. If you bought into this agenda of slamming free speech, you accepted low consciousness. Why on earth would you *ever* do that?

Who can hardly wait for the truths to come out? All of us. All I can say is that those who took a sentimental journey, following the heart's yearnings, will find they are on a very different track from some others. Those who did harm, who cheated people, and who rigged elections around the world will have to answer to the engineer who is driving the train. He has a three-letter word on his badge: G-O-D.

Beyond Fear

*"I don't believe that expressing your opinion,
regardless of who is there, is being rude. And
it is shame that we've reached a level in our
country where we think that you don't have
the right to put your opinion out there."*
—Benjamin Carson

We all had the opportunity to state our opinions. We could have held strong to our freedom and liberty and stated our opinions. When interpersonal dynamics got too sensitive, we could have shut off the television, radio, and social media. Too many people thought the world was coming to an end. When our fears take over our reality, it manipulates our thought patterns. Some people started thinking they were going to die in a pandemic; that the year 2020 was bound to be their soul's end. Come on! If that was you, you slacked in your judgment and your faith in humanity. Since when did you decide to become a victim? Victim energy is the worst kind of energy. It is very dark; it breeds unstable people and actions. This is another soul truth. Please take note.

Let me take you out of your comfortable sandbox for a moment with this story. It has to do with why people and cultures choose to be victims, and it will help you understand why you should not become one. My friend Larry Peacock, MD, shared this concept with me, and when I heard it, I had a lightbulb/Tesla moment! Larry and I were discussing what makes people see themselves as victims.

"Many people lose their hunt," Larry said.

I was curious and asked what he meant.

He said, "Animals never, ever quit, do they? They never see themselves losing or going hungry. It is in their nature to always take care of themselves."

Think of a fox. If it is hungry for dinner and misses out on the first rabbit it goes after, it doesn't miss a meal, complain there is no food, or call the government to provide its food that day. No! The fox keeps hunting until it has the best rabbit it can find. It never gives up the hunt. The fox gets up the next day and does it all over again. We humans? Many people stopped hunting. Did you give up your hunt in 2020 and 2021?

People need to shift in order to create their own opportunity. We can always find our way around obstacles, and because of that, we never need to give up on ourselves, we never need to give up "the hunt." Think about the business owner whose business failed or was lost during the pandemic but who found other work. Or the underdog athlete who became a Super Bowl champion. Or the person suffering from a challenging medical disease who never gave up and eventually overcame it. People like this did not give up on their hunt; like hungry foxes, they kept hunting.

Don't give up. Spirit is yelling, "Get back to your hunt!"

Prayer

*"I used to believe that prayer changes
things, but now I know that prayer
changes us, and we change things."*
—Mother Teresa

Spirit has been there every step of the way for us during the pandemic and in all times of great crisis. Spirit tells us, "You will be safe." Spirit told you to pray (which many of you did), to pay attention to the details, and to notice the synchronicity of events. Spirit asked you to question the truth and agendas of politicians and media outlets. Intuition was on fire! People prayed for their fellow man. During this pandemic, people prayed who had never prayed before. That is a miracle in itself! Our whole world had a common goal, which is pretty amazing, if you ask me. The situation showed all of us that humanity can be harmonious even when the world is in chaos. I am here to remind you that the Spirit within you was nudging you to hunt again and again and again.

We have never been given so much spiritual motivation to trust our own judgment. Sadly, though, many people bought into fear-based data and messages. Many of you bought into the idea that you, personally, were going to die from the pandemic, and that was far from the truth. My guides want you to know that you had a 99 percent chance of survival if you got this disease. Sadly, many people forgot to evoke the good and align with the light energy of God. Everything is a transmission of light for your body, mind, and soul. The Divine holds that vibration. It's what makes you feel good about yourself or, if you are not in alignment, negative about yourself. It's how you think. It's how you treat others. If you are being a nasty person and treating others without compassion, the universe will give that behavior right back to you. Karma keeps score, and you want the good karma on your team, not the other one. It's also about how you speak to yourself. So, think about the great things you add to this life, not the missed opportunities. It's a pretty simple. Think and accept only the good. When you become fearful, you vibrate at a lower consciousness, so don't go there or you will bring harm upon yourself. Be all about the good alignment, as that brings in your joy.

If you allowed fear, you killed your own energy vibration before it could help you stay healthy and whole, and for what? Who goes to the Super Bowl telling themselves they are going to lose the game? Not one player, coach, or team staff member *would ever* think those thoughts. The goal of a sports team is to win (remember the W for Win?) But in this "pandemic game," the unknown was kicking people's asses before they even got onto the field!

When the pandemic hit, everyone should have showed up to play the most important game of our time and with a perfect record (a great immune system). Maybe you were that Super Bowl player, fighting off dis-ease in your community. Many people saw it as a perfect storm. To witness the despair, you only had to hit a few social media sites or watch the hysteria hitting your friends and family. So many people were fear-based, and so the pandemic became their perfect storm. Others rose high above fear. Many of you *did not*, and you lost that game before your cleats even touched the turf!

Did you really believe the virus was going to kill you? Think about it. Only the Lord knows the timing of our death, so during the crisis, I did not let my energy move in that direction. For two years, I did not think that or feel that, and I did not give my body any inkling of it. I prayed for the collective, as so many healers and others did. I prayed that people would be able to shift their doomsday thoughts.

2020 showed us who we would want on our island if we were shipwrecked. The funny thing is, in truth, no one was ever alone in any of it. God was with us, and our intuition was available in every circumstance we encountered. You just had to let it in to be comforted or let it lead you into your *flow* to get your best outcome.

> *"You have Brains in Your Head. You have Feet*
> *in Your Shoes. You can Steer yourself any*
> *Direction You Choose."*
> —Dr. Seuss

Letting Go of Hate

*"An eye for an eye will only make
the whole world blind."*
—Mahatma Gandhi

"I am healed, I am whole." I say these words daily as a reminder of who I am and who I want to become. Your wholeness comes from the words you say to yourself daily, because they affect every part of your day. Your hate also affects every part of your day because it aligns your energy with hostage and harm. Would you prefer love and harmony or hostage and harm? You get to pick. Hate energy brings chaos and saps your strength. Have you observed the state of the world, lately? Everyone has an agenda, and the agenda is all about control. We all have felt this because so many people have welcomed it. It's really rather gross. Think of a destructive relationship: you keep going back for more of the same. Smarten up and don't do it. Change your pattern.

Even if you are tired of the hate, you still have to see the lesson. Hate digs deep into your soul. It's like Silly String that pops out of a can. The string keeps going and going and then, in the end, there's no one but you to pick up the mess on the ground. I gave out that party favor at a kid's party one time. Never again. In mid-winter, I found that string in the yard from a spring party!

Hate is similar to Silly String that has been pushed down deep: just when you think it's gone, there it is again. This is why you have to deal with hate properly. You have to clear out your hate and the hate that comes from those who are harming you with their hate. Two words tell us how to manage hate: release it.

I can tell you that Spirit is working hard to help us with *all* of our human errors related to hate, and the bottom line is this: hatred will *not* serve you, your country, or your world. Hatred will lead you to nowhere good. When we leave this earth plane, we will have to answer for our soul choices. Believe me, it is so much easier to work in kindness. Kindness is the better plan. Remember, we are all about premium roses, a big bouquet, not weeds. Choose love. Love will bring you peace. If you have the capacity for hate, you should have the same capacity for love. If you don't, I suggest you do some major internal healing. When you are healed from hate, your inward self will thank you.

> *"Hate, it has caused a lot of problems in the world, but it has not solved one yet."*
> —Maya Angelou

Every day in 2020 and 2021, I have sent healing to myself and my family. I would then send it to our president, our country, and our world, in that order. I manifested that healing and *flow*, and I trusted what my guidance gave me.

Honestly, there was no other choice. I would not let fear come into my thoughts. Did you let in fear? Too many people in this world did, and that is awful. They fell out of *flow* and right into chaos, which led to hate.

It is time to move on, but it is difficult to change. Hate has such a strong memory—no dementia there. Remember in the midst of your stress to always forgive the hate that comes up. This little act will make you whole in your presence, one with what your soul is supposed to fulfill in this lifetime. This situation is telling us that maybe our souls have to mature a bit. Hey, I know it is hard to love the haters, but once you start—wow, will your world change! Your intuitive mind will grow and grow and grow.

It is important for you begin viewing your internal self as being just as important as your external self. You need to outwardly accept. We all know that what is happening externally in our lives seems to matter more—the house, the career, the golf score. Yes, all those things can bring some happiness, but the inner you, your soul, is what brings you into your true divinity. This energy is what ushers in your completeness and creates your wisdom.

> *"What lies behind us and what lies before us are tiny matters compared to what lies within us."*
> —Oliver Wendell Holmes

I am no different and the world is no different because of these past challenges. Spirit wants to tell you that *you* are no different, either. So, if you have been playing the victim and gravitating into that dark energy—stop. Enough, now. We are all quite similar in what we want— love, love, and more love. Peace, peace, and more peace. Health, health, and more health. Wealth, wealth, and more wealth. Liberty, liberty, and more liberty. Freedom, freedom, and more freedom.

Individually, you can create this kind of fulfillment. Better yet, you can create fulfillment globally just by changing your thought patterns. It works like magic when you actively take part in the collective consciousness. Every day, you can pray to God to take the evil off this planet and beg God/Nature to protect the good in humankind. It is amazing what our thoughts can do. It's time to switch it up with your thoughts. Envision the good every day. Can you imagine the outcome for the world if we all did this?

It is time to introduce new thoughts into your life. Switching from fear to healthy thought patterns takes you beyond the limits of your consciousness, and that can only give you peace and manifest greater wisdom. Now, who ain't about that! You will gain a profound understanding of God, the Spirit within you, blended with the capacity of love and attuned to your own likeness, which is your goodness.

The universe conspires to give you what you want. It always will. It will wreck all the evil in this world. With Spirit, your intuition is powerful. Just trust it to do the good that it is meant to do. Create a higher intention for yourself, and the rest will follow. Don't, and I repeat *don't,* let yourself be pulled into dark energy. Keep your energy light so that it can evolve through your good intentions and hold on to the people who nurture your heart even amidst the storms.

I am no superhero, and neither are you, but through all the trials that came with the pandemic, there were moments when I'm sure we all felt that superhero energy. Our lives were chaotic, the world was chaotic, and life was hard and sad, but, like many people, I was determined not to let my *flow* be undermined. There were certainly moments when my psychic net held me like a new baby with a pacifier in its mouth. It held you, too, and it was never going to let you go, the suction was so tight. Way too many people dropped their *flow* during this time, and some will continue to choose that lower vibration in the future. Please, don't be one of them. Those are the people we need to help. If you see someone going down that dark path, remind them how valuable they are. Encourage those souls to wake up to their inner guidance so that they can make better decisions.

Intuitive Leadership

"You know the truth by the way it feels."
—Unknown

Look at where we are today. See how far we have come. In less than a year after the onset of the pandemic, vaccines were being created at warp speed. And now, common drugs used for other illnesses are assisting with the symptoms, so that if you get Covid-19 and Sars-2, you have a 99 percent chance of survival. We can now logically say that this virus is not as frightening as we all thought it was. It does not mean sure death. We know where it originated. The cure rate is extremely high and, best of all, children have a stronger immunity to it. Thank you, God! We know who the vulnerable population is, so we protect them and help them to stay safe. Isn't it amazing that the medical world has achieved such grand goals? I think so. I am also thankful for the research and discovery that are taking place in medicine. It shows us that miracles can occur. It also has shown us how prevention good vitamins and your own immunity is a powerful superhero quality to this disease.

This pandemic has educated you. If you chose to listen to your instinct, then you questioned whether an inoculation felt right for you. You looked at statistics and narratives to make your awareness sync with your decision for your body, all a personal choice. Remember, your body is always your own kingdom and no one else's. God really did make you perfect. Don't forget that message when it comes to your body healing itself. Your own immunity is the ultimate powerhouse of your kingdom. Be wise and treat it well.

Remember, we have to look backwards to go forward. We can be thankful to science and medicine that they didn't go into fear mode. They drove that pandemic ship through rough seas and came out ahead. Why? Because they trusted their instinct and, I would hope, trusted Spirit. Intuition increased in all of us during 2020 and 2021. By the grace of God medical personnel, scientists, and most world leaders were guided to help humanity. We must remember that infections will always be a part of our world. This is nothing new, and it is certainly not going to change. Our bodies are the real superwomen and supermen of this crisis healing. God created our bodies to heal themselves daily. It is okay to be exposed to germs. Why? Because germs give us natural immunity so that our bodies can do their job. God made an amazing product!

Herd immunity is a beautiful thing. Building your immunity is a beautiful thing. I am old enough to remember chickenpox parties. Are you? Those particular play dates were meant to make sure you got infected with chickenpox. We kids would compare how many spots we ended up with. No parent or kid was too afraid of chickenpox because they trusted their bodies to take care of themselves and inhibit the disease. News flash! Your body did the right thing by you during this pandemic, too. It is no different today. When you get sick, you can affirm that your body is healed and whole. You can believe that Spirit within you is capable of healing itself. During this pandemic, we sadly forgot about chickenpox parties and how amazing our bodies are. Our bodies can take on disease and give us immunity. Damn straight! Our bodies can get the W for the Win.

> *"The heavy is the root of the light. The unmoved us the source of all movement. Thus, the master travels all day without leaving home. However splendid the views, she stays serenely in herself. Why should the lord of the country flit about like a fool? If you let yourself be blown to and fro, you lose touch with your root. If you let restlessness move you, you lose touch with who you are."*
> —Lao-Tzu, Tao-te-Ching

In my opinion, Lau-Tzu's statement can be applied to what has occurred during this pandemic. We have been challenged to trust our own bodies. We have also seen the leadership in our communities, our states, and our country fail. Many leaders in government should be ashamed of the ego and narcissism they have shown in choosing to harm their fellow man. Karma has a good memory. She can land a pretty good left hook just when you least expect it. In the next twenty months, you are going to see so much revealed. The true facts of this pandemic are beginning to come out, and we will see that it could have been managed much better. In the meantime, what else can we do but wait for evidence and pray for solidarity and strength? But most important, pay attention to your intuition, as it will yield valuable information.

During this pandemic, did you accept and buy into the fear? Did you question what the media was telling you? Did you question authority? Or did something in that instinct of yours say, "Is this really right?" I don't gamble, but I would bet your instinct, your psychic net, told you to question what you were hearing and to trust in what felt right to Y-O U. That may be the only good thing to come out of the pandemic. Our psychic ability has urged us not to make choices with just our heads or just our hearts, but by blending head and heart so that you can trust your intuition. Can you give me a hallelujah?

Our psychic ability has urged us not to make choices with just our heads or just our hearts, but by blending head and heart so that you can trust your intuition.

Spirit within was speaking and sometimes screaming at you during 2020 and 2021. God has given you some great goods to work with—remember that. Human beings truly are perfect, or at least we all start out that way. When we pay attention, we instinctively know what is right for our own bodies and immune systems and our safety. Because of the world crisis, this cool, newfound vibration is here to stay, and it will work with your soul from here on out. The energy of 2021 and 2022 has emerged, and it is all about liberty and freedom and doing what feels right for you.

Remember that this energy is yours, so what do you want to do with it? This is your time to change physically, mentally, and energetically. Let freedom ring!

Freedom and Liberty

"Freedom is the oxygen of the soul."
—Moshe Dayan

Freedom and liberty are rights of the soul, period. From now on, you will be urged from within not to allow restrictive energy within you or around you. People, places, and things that no longer align with your personal space simply can't be in it, "and so it is and will be." Humans who try to mess with that truth will find the old patterns breaking up quickly. They will be quite surprised at what hits them. Spirit has defined this for me. It will apply on the personal, political, and global levels. These are important times to learn from. 2021 through 2023 will offer the same opportunities for growth as 2020, with lots of ups and downs. So, it is important to be grounded and to focus on what aligns with you. Remember, that freedom is your right as a human being! With all this growth, we will all be about ten feet tall when we are "done and dusted." When 2023 arrives, there will be no fear in anyone. Do you hear me?

That space of Spirit and psychic connection and inner knowing is truly sacred. Unlike the old fear-based meaning of "safe space," this is the real "safe space." The experiences you have when you connect to your source are real. Please stop thinking that they are not.

In my readings for clients, I hear the ways that Spirit talks to them. If only they had listened, their circumstances could have been different. I hear these stories every day. I truly love how people are understanding and embracing their newfound kinship to connection. Today, many people truly are aligning with their own, new Bill of Rights the soul kind of rights. You know, the ones you came to this earth to understand. This is why, energetically, you feel your power and rights being taken away from you. Your soul is giving you a message: you are the one in power, guided by God. This combination will bless your life with good choices and abundance. Be willing to accept change and be open to the new, but don't forget to cherish your past. Your history has taught you some great lessons. You cannot erase history, but you can move forward from it to do things differently.

History has energy. *Everything* has energy. History always teaches but you can never erase it or pretend it didn't happen. Remember my line, "Spirit always makes me look backward to go forward." This is how to gain perspective. As you look at poor life choices, don't throw fear into the mix, just learn to do better next time.

We are going to go back in time for a moment to a lesson your mother taught you. As kids, we all managed to manipulate the cookie jar. Think of yourself as a four-year-old who got caught eating a cookie before dinner, and your mother is doing the big cookie bust on you. Mom reprimands you so you don't spoil your dinner. You learn to respect Mom's wishes and learn not to cheat. Then, you eat a good dinner, and she rewards you at the end with a cookie for dessert to reinforce her point. Mother taught you two things: to listen and not to cheat. Even at four, you understand that, if you don't cheat, tomorrow night's lovingly made chicken nuggets and fries will get you that sweet reward. History teaches us great lessons even when we are very young.

History is meant to show us a new direction. We can still learn from our current lessons; we can learn not to repeat them. This applies to both forbidden cookies or to world events. You can't erase history; you can only change your behavior to make it different.

When I see these organizations taking down statues and trying to destroy monuments, I want to say, "Hello—news flash! This is *not* going to change anything energetically!" Energy is past, present, and future, and it stays forever. You will never eliminate the energy, even if you take down the monument. The space where the monument was still holds that energy. If only the world would sit back and ponder that a bit.

As a world, we should have no fear, so we can recognize our past and learn from it. As my Father said to me once, "We sacrifice to make the next generation better and we always learn from our past never forget that Kel." I never have. My father was that World War II generation went into the Navy at age seventeen and never graduated from high school. He became a very accomplished man, but he always wanted more for his children. It's time to make humankind a little more brilliant. Everyone needs to understand that history can be harsh, but it is there to teach us to do our lives differently and that is a good thing. As Albert said…

"Energy never disappears from the universe."
—Albert Einstein

The Political Side of the Pandemic and What Spirit Thinks

"Our scientific power has outrun our spiritual power. We have guided missiles and misguided men."
—Martin Luther King, Jr.

Was there a political side to this pandemic? You bet there was! Many countries had false narratives. Did they use the pandemic for election fraud, economic gain, and to control citizens through censorship? Of course, they did. We all saw it or felt it personally. I never, ever thought we would see such a thing in my lifetime. But it did happen, and it will continue. We haven't learned the lesson about stealing from the cookie jar. Unfortunately, this situation is not happening just between a parent and a child. It is happening among countries and among citizens. Energetically, it is disturbing, and everyone can feel it. It is so out of character for humanity to be confined.

Have you felt the confinement? I know you have, and I am reminding you that your Spirit guides are protecting you, right now. A unique vibration is occurring to conquer nasty behavior create a better good for this world. God, your guides, your guardian angels, and your loved ones who have passed are all behind it. All I can say is that the higher dimensions have humanity's back. That lower plane of energy we are witnessing, and all that malicious behavior will come to a sudden halt. Better get prepared. I have never felt such intense energy from the other side. It is trying to correct such errors. Many psychic mediums I know have felt the same.

When something does not feel right, listen to your energy. It is 100-percent correct. Spirit within you is trying hard to get your attention. It's okay to react in healthy ways for the betterment of humanity, but humanity is tilting into conscious control over society. Spirit is saying, "We've got a problem, people!" Humanity is like two men battling a great white shark over who is going to become breakfast in the morning. This is what you are witnessing presently.

Remember, 2021 through 2023 represent two words and two words *only:* freedom and liberty. Your job is to go and find yours. Find out what freedom and liberty mean in your life, your community, your country, and our world. When you work within the scope of the energies of freedom and liberty good outcomes happen. Remember, you are a leader, not a follower. If you understand liberty and freedom, you will be "all good" in your personal dynamics. In 2020, my ninety-one-year-old mother said more than once, "Kelle, what on earth are people thinking these days? This world has gone crazy." Boy, how *right* my dear old mom was.

Albert Einstein comes in with the best quote ever for this subject:

"Only two things are infinite, the universe and human stupidity, and I'm not so sure about the universe."

The power of the ego is way out of control in political leadership. Worldwide, we have seen scandal after scandal worldwide. All of this is being unveiled on a daily basis. Spirit says, "Pay attention. Administrations trying to erase presidential legacies? Hello, we have all lived and benefited from those legacies, and now you are telling us what happened didn't happen? Come on! Do you think the soul is that stupid? It certainly is not. But the ego is that stupid. Who else feels like we are living in the *Godfather* movie? I sure do. I keep thinking of that line from the movie: "Someday, and that day may never come, I will call upon you to do a service for me."

How many fraudulent deals have taken place during this pandemic? How many people who could work chose not to work because they felt entitled to government assistance, and still do? How many elections around the world are just now being proven fraudulent by expert analysis? It has left the world aghast! These things have happened everywhere—just name a country and name an event. Were you paying attention when your Spirit guides told you that something was off? I hope no one was asking you for any favors!

SPIRIT SPEAKS WITHIN YOU

When I was burying my mother in June of 2020, the funeral director told us they were getting car accident victims to embalm whose cause of death was listed as Covid-19. What? Wouldn't you think funeral homes would know the difference between a body from a car crash and a body that had died from a blood-clotting lung disease? Me, too. Were states making money off this pandemic? That's the real question. Did they have to keep their Covid-19 death numbers elevated for a reason? Did someone call in, "just a few services," like the line from the Godfather?

I have to wonder just how many more service requests were called in so states could present their fraud. People get really angry when they remember how nursing homes were handled and the high death rates for the elderly and physically disabled. And how about the neglect that happened in veteran homes? I have done readings for families whose parents were beaten up by staff members. How did they find out about this neglect? Through an outside window during a visit to that trusted home.

Those families could not go into the facilities and get their parents out because of the state mandates. Imagine the fear of all these vulnerable people, and that includes the families left on the outside. I have done readings for families where patients' DNR (Do Not Resuscitate) preferences were not followed. The patient wanted to be kept alive, and the hospital broke the law. Here is a newsflash from Spirit. If you wanted to make money off of illness or create strife and sadness for your fellow man— Spirit has your number.

*"Sooner or later, everyone sits down to
a banquet of consequences."*
—Robert Louis Stevenson

Get Out Your Psychic Press Release

"Re-examine all you have been told.
Dismiss what insults your soul."
—Walt Whitman

I find myself looking at world events from a psychic perspective, and you should. When I work a missing-person case, I send out my psychic press release and ask, "Who? What? When? Where? How?" I do the same regarding the events of the last two years. You should be doing the same. I asked these questions about the legitimacy of elections, not just in the US, but around the world. Many elections were showing numbers for a win that just could not be statistically accurate. Once again, I looked to the *Godfather* movies for answers, and I have to agree with another line from the movie: "I don't trust society to protect us. I have no intention of placing fate in the hands of men whose only qualification is that they managed to con a block of people to vote for them."

If you don't con and do illegal favors these days, I think you are going to be A-Okay, but sadly some misguided people have been up to no good for way too long, and that has wreaked havoc on our blessed world. We have seen this, and most important, we have felt it energetically. When the major collective of people feels the same thing you do, you know Spirit agrees with you. You, my friend, are 100-percent correct!"

Millions upon millions of people cannot have the same inclination and evidence and not be accurate. Remember the example of the Three Wise Men? They gave you the holy trinity of psychic prowess. They are with you now more than ever. Use their services! It's like having a new, psychic BMW sitting in your driveway. Don't just look at it. It's time to grab the damn keys and take it for a spin!

Spirit wants you to question things. Look for validation. Don't just rely on what you've been told about that BMW. Drive that car and evaluate how she performs. Put out your own psychic press release. Start digging deep for answers and watch how the Spirit energy provides them. It's amazing. Once you dive into that practice, your whole world changes. I ask you not to just use these tools during world catastrophes. Ask questions daily, and then sit back and listen to what your intuition is telling you. Your inner self will bloom like never before, and your independent thinking will begin.

The World Is Round, Not Flat

Greek scholars like Pythagoras and Aristotle proved that the world was round and not flat. Christopher Columbus believed this, too. He knew it to be true, and he never fell off the edge of the earth while traveling. Then, in the year 1828, Washington Irving wrote a fictional biography of Columbus: *The Life and Voyages of Christopher Columbus*. It became a bestseller. However, Irving was a storyteller (think *Rip Van Winkle* and *The Legend of Sleepy Hollow*). He put his spin on the story to make it more interesting. He wrote that Columbus took his journey to prove the opposite of what was true. Guess what happened.

People believed it. That piece of fiction changed people's perception of why Columbus set off on his journey. False facts covered up the truth. Columbus's reputation was tarnished by someone wanting a bestseller. Today, we would call it fake news/media propaganda— nonsense, fact-less stories for ratings. Sadly, too many people today are compromising their belief systems; they're not looking for the legitimate facts. Some are choosing to be guided by today's storytellers instead of researching the facts for themselves. Spirit is giving you this example to remind you to think for yourself. Don't be misled.

The world has always been round and not flat. Scholars discovered this long before Columbus. You should not believe everything you hear or read these days. If news organizations or administrations are canceling facts, ask yourself why. When you hear or read a news story, ask your intuition whether it feels right. Get into the Who, What, When, Where, and How of these stories. You will know intuitively whether they are storytelling or real facts. It is time to trust your instinct about what you read in articles or listen to on the world news.

In 1828, fake news was happening, too, just to sell a few more books for Irving. This example was given by Spirit to remind you to think for yourself and to never ever be misled. Today, it is important to keep your world round, not flat. Do you see the point?

Signs

"Pay attention to the signs all around you, for your way is being lighted by the power of the universe and the love of all the spirits around you. There is so much support for you."
—Sandra Ingerman

I am a big believer in signs. Noticing signs from beyond is the easiest way to connect to Spirit, and to your loved ones who have passed, for comfort and validation. Here is how.

First, ask a question. Then, tell your guides or loved one that you are expecting them to give you a particular sign as a confirmation to your question, and then wait. You will see your sign as an indication of the direction you are meant to go. Here is an example; "If I am meant to switch jobs, I want to see Charlie Brown, the cartoon character from the "Peanuts" gang. Before you know it, you will see the Charlie Brown character, hear the name Charlie, or maybe hear the last name Brown. If you are not meant to switch jobs at this time, you won't see or hear anything like that. Even better yet, you start your new position, and your co-worker is named Charley, and she is the girl that you end up marrying!

That's right, *you* tell your guides the sign you want to see. Make that sign different and playful so you will remember it. Spirit sees this little exercise as part of your *flow,* and this is how you can begin to connect with them. Remember, your Three Wise Men, your holy trinity of psychic prowess. They are helping you link with your loved ones. At some point, you will get so good at connecting that you won't even need energetic help. Are you ready for the transformation?

Our world is one big *vibration.* Like a rock skipping across a pond, you vibrate the world with your energy, creating a ripple effect on the atmosphere and blending it into our world. The cause and effect of vibration is based on human choices that align with the positive or align with the negative. When it comes to energy, there is no taking the Switzerland route of neutrality. You have to pick a side. Every energy, positive or negative, creates a ripple effect. Spirit says, "You are a stone creating ripples of energy on the world."

Remember, you are a soul here on this earth plane. If some narrative does not feel right, go internal and focus on that. Just think of yourself and what you need to heal. Don't get all caught up with the world stage. What's on that stage, my friend, possibly had a different agenda all along. From my psychic perspective, I see accountability for others on many, many levels. Instead of attracting the toxic vibrations of others, stick to your own agenda and no other to keep your vibration higher and cleaner. This objective can be really difficult to achieve, but I know you can manage it. Remember, in this lifetime, you were born to handle it.

Spirit says, "You are a stone creating ripples of energy on the world."

We have talked about the *Godfather* movies, and now we are going to click the remote and switch to a new movie, *The Blues Brothers*. Today, I want you to be like Elwood and Jake. One of my favorite lines from the movie is when Elwood says, "We're on a mission from God."

You are on a mission from God, too! You are being called to act and be part of your divine sovereignty to yourself and your community. It is your soul's job to beam your light, not to fall prey to the darkness of evil.

Who Am I?

"Who am I? Not knowing this is the greatest death to the Soul (one's own self)!"
—Dada Bhagwan

You need to grab the collective playbook of your ascension as a soul and ask yourself the question, "Who am I?" Are you ready to accept your own divinity? I have been working on that for years. Many people have been doing this, including you. The time to create your future is—like yesterday! We have such short windows of time to complete things. Don't miss them by waiting until next year or even three months from now. Our spiritual guidance is ready, waiting for you to wake up. You and your guidance are going to be a real power couple, knocking it out of the park, no amateurs allowed. Please don't align with the negative. It places you in a space of great harm. Instead, from here on out, focus on your own actions and attitude. It is the safest route for your liberation and for your ascension. It is time to stop worrying about everyone else and take care of you, addressing your whole mind, body, and Spirit.

How you adjust your vibration now will set the tone for your next few decades. Yes, we are planning twenty years out, a long time. It's time to embody this change and shift into your soul level. Remember, we are all just souls. These dynamic times are here to remind us to get back into alignment with Spirit within. Anyone up for some healing? It's about to occur. These dramatic changes are about to turn us to the next page. We are in a time that is focused on creating great solutions and not on letting doubt betray us.

How do you liberate your own freedoms and rights? You download them into your Spiritual consciousness. You start instantly to change into that new soul you are meant to be in the next few years. These are epic times for human transformation. I say it's about time you start addressing your soul's bylaws. Do you know what they are? Ask questions.

- **What are my life goals?**
- **What are my spiritual goals?**
- **What are my intuitive goals?**
- **How will Spirit within work with me?**

Those answers are your soul's bylaws. Write them down. If you don't define your soul's bylaws, you will live blindly and continue to find chaos. Spirit within you needs this new direction. You are the only one who can define it, and this is how you will achieve it.

The definition of chaos is complete disorder and confusion. Don't go there if you can help it.

In the last few decades, we have had some crazy dynamics. Many ideologies will be unveiled in 2021 through 2023. You will have to stay strong in your belief system. And most important, every day, channel your inner Blues Brothers and "Remember the mission."

Blame

"When you think everything is someone else's fault, you suffer a lot. When you realize everything springs only from yourself, you will learn both peace and joy."
—Dalai Lama

Did you look for someone to blame for this pandemic instead of looking at the facts of how it started? Did you ever ask your intuition or your Spirit guides why it happened? I'll bet not, so I ask you to dive in and find those answers, now. People have become more intuitive during this crisis. This luminous energy is part of the agenda. The "Great Awakening," that's what this time is about. Our souls are not pushing the snooze button and being lazy. They are getting up and starting fresh. If any good came out of this pandemic, it is this: Spirit is yelling at those who are still sleeping to get up! Remember your Mom in the mornings before school started? Yep, like that.

Here is the newest memo from Spirit: "No more blame games. Accept responsibility for your actions and stop pointing your fingers at others because this happened to you. Blaming gets you nowhere. It's time for you to be accountable. You have to accept that your actions can really screw you up. Get back to your *flow*. At the end of the day, it is just you and Spirit. You came into this world with your life lessons, and in death you leave with them, also. You need to keep your life simple, and all will flow nicely. And when achievement doesn't leave you humble, give that some credence, too.

Humble means giving a modest or low estimate (ouch!) of our own importance.

We are in a time of reflection. To create peace on earth, make peace in your own home and your own heart. We have to fix ourselves. We have to stop hating and stop enjoying the victim role so much. To create a healthy world of consciousness, stop sacrificing your own mental health for other people: that is a first step.

Remember the scene in *The Blues Brothers* movie where Elwood is on stage at the Palace Hotel Ballroom? He knows they are in big trouble. When the police show up, this is how Elwood handles the room:

"We're so glad to see so many people here tonight. And we would especially like to welcome the representatives of the Illinois law enforcement community that have chosen to join us here in the Palace Hotel Ballroom at this time. We certainly hope you all enjoy the show. And remember, people, that no matter who you are and what you do to live, thrive, and survive, there are still some things that make us all the same. You. Me. Them. Everybody. Everybody."

We are that *everybody*.

If you make the choice to *flow*, guess what? You will. Sure, you might hit a bump in the road, as my mom and dad would say. Spirit is saying that you are super-strong, and your psychic net is right there to protect you—I promise. I see it time and time again. I could tell you story after story of how Spirit has worked with clients. Remember, I have been doing readings for almost eighteen years, now. If this gal doesn't know how *flow*/Spirit works, I should change careers or go back into real estate.

Today, my real estate is Spirit and grabbing all those house listings (you). My career is to help *everybody* understand their own psychic ability. When you dive into the victim culture and enjoy blaming others, ugly words like threat, defeat, anxiety, and anger fill your consciousness. If you allow yourself to become a casualty of this low, low vibration, you can easily lose your opportunity for prosperity. I wouldn't gamble that for anything, but then again, I'm a penny-slot girl.

Life Path

"Who you are tomorrow begins
with what you do today."
—Tim Fargo

I am pretty good at this energy stuff, as the psychic net has made *me* its life's work. I say this because no one raises their hand to be a psychic medium. Truly, this work picks you. I have often imagined God giving me my soul path as I was being born, and right before I entered the world, He yelled out, "Oh, yeah, Kelle, I forgot to mention that you are going to be a psychic medium. Surprise! I didn't have a chance to question that choice. In life, sometimes we don't get to debate. We just have to accept our fate. I truly love what I do. I know my path defines me. I just love to connect for others. This work is my passion, and I have built the best psychic marriage. But this work can be challenging for people who do not understand it.

I could not have done this service for over eighteen years without having been shown proof of the validity of Spirit and intuition. This intuition gift works in *everyone*. I know you have felt the presence of a loved one or have asked for guidance and received it. Psychic ability is simple because it is just that, simple. You do not need to fear its strength; just embrace the confirmations it always gives you. Your intuitive gifts are mighty if they are used for your highest and best good. Trust them. Look at a US quarter. What does it say? "In God We Trust." Signs from Spirit are everywhere. Look for them and acknowledge them.

You can expand your faith through belief in your own psychic ability. Spirit within you gives this gift every single day, and you don't even think about it. You are one hot ticket in your expertise as a professional, as a parent, as a child, as a friend, and as a soul with God. It is time to notice the signs you are given and your inner guidance. This can yield valuable information, but only if you pay attention. I know many of you have done this, and some of you are works in progress. I absolutely love that about you.

How can you get better at listening to your intuition? Just follow my lead:

- Your first assignment is to be *brave* in your choices.
- The second assignment is to be *present*. You are not to think of yesterday or your past or your future. Just be present right now to what you can accomplish in clairvoyance.
- Finally, *trust* what you receive. If you have conviction, *flow* always completes itself. If you second guess yourself, you have just botched it, so no second-guessing.

Now, you begin manifesting. You will never fear decision-making again. I tell you, if you can embody this trilogy of bravery, presence, and trust, you have made it to the level of true soul guidance. Wow! Your life is now going to embrace the utmost in possibilities! I am excited for you. You are meant to do great things.

Embrace Your Psychic Self

The Universe is saying: "Allow me to flow through you unrestricted, and you will see the greatest magic you have ever seen."
—Klaus Joehle

Your psychic *flow* can feel as natural as putting on a pair of shoes every day. Now, I know some men are not too creative in that department. Us gals, though, we watch out for our feet because we know how shoes can really pop an outfit. Paying attention to your psychic *flow* is just like that—it feels good, it looks good, and it has the "it" factor. When you use your psychic intuition and you are listening and *flowing*, it's like wearing shoes that fit perfectly. Nothing feels better! If you are not inviting that psychic ability to fulfill you, then you are wearing the wrong size shoes. It's like your feet are slipping around and being pinched and you are developing a blister on your heel. Energy blistering does not sit well. Being out of balance means emotional pain and sometimes physical pain. It is now time to find the ideal shoes for you.

Your energy wants to fit into the perfect size for you. That shoe may come in a cute kitten pump or a black sexy boot, or it could be a sturdy Birkenstock sandal—whatever makes you feel good. Energy comes in lots of styles and sizes. It just has to fit so your guidance can work with you. The bottom line is this: fill your shoes with Spirit. Like the old saying goes, "If the shoe fits, wear it." I am telling you that Spirit is sizing you up and is reminding you that you are the only person who can fill those shoes.

Your agenda is simple: it's just you and your feet embracing your psychic self. Your feet take you in good directions, now, don't they? I write that, laughing. Your feet take you places and so does your Spirit guidance. So, where are you going?

- Who will be with you?
- Will you make space for your spirituality?
- Will you make space for love, dignity, and trust?
- Will you give back to others that love, dignity, and trust you receive?

Your *flow* always includes others. My *flow* lives by this mantra. In fact, there is a sign in my house that reads, "The hand that gives, gathers." That is Spirit within you. It is walking your talk right now.

Life has so many facets. It is in love that we live best without sorrow, for nothing we love is ever lost. When you give to someone, you feel all that good emotion. As you live this way, Spirit within you will bloom into stunning roses and become your permanent bouquet. In this time of great changes, you really need to hear this message. I hope you will understand it and, most important, act on it.

> *It is in love that we live best without sorrow,*
> *for nothing we love is ever lost.*

All of these anecdotes from Spirit mean one thing: you need to embrace your instinctual *flow* from God. Once you do, you will recognize it and never fight it again. Your shoes will fit perfectly.

How do you embrace your Spirit *flow*? It's as simple as getting quiet. Can you imagine that key word becoming part of your vocabulary and your life? *Quiet.* I don't know about you, but the older I get, the more I need quiet. Ask yourself, does your environment and do the people around you own you? Can you stop pleasing everyone? Because, if nothing else, your pleasing is creating crutches that get in the way of everyone's growth. Get into your own safe space where no one and nothing owns you. *You* are the only safe space needed.

No one can be in your safe space but you. You own that place, so cuddle up with a cup of tea or take a walk alone. It is your time all for yourself before you make dinner or do errands or go to work. You have earned it. Then show your loved ones how to create their own private space. Your job is to show them the value of quiet, especially your children.

When you find time to relax during your day, turn the phone off as well as the people around you off (some of you may take great pleasure in this), you become harmony for your soul. I know most of you don't take alone time daily. In fact, most people are pretty bad at creating that time for themselves. If you want to be psychic, then stop multitasking every hour of the day. You have to find your cup of calm every day so that guidance can come to you. You need peace in your day to grow your soul.

Messages from Spirit do not come through kinetic energy, so stop being so kinetic! It is a choice. You need to quit living like an airplane in turbulence with all those bumps, fears, and forgetting to breathe! Sure, it can be scary to make a change, but you're the pilot. You can "boot up" a few thousand feet and find the smooth air. Why don't you? Do you like the daily turbulence? Remind me what the name of your airline is. I won't be taking it.

You will need peace so you can listen to Spirit and get a message. You need a clear channel to work with and no "airplane potholes" to contend with. My little kids used to call them that. They also loved what they called the "roller coaster rides" during landing. As for me, I was thinking something more like, "What the *truck*" on those flights.

I have always loved the Serenity Prayer. Say this when you are having a disconnected day. It will heal your emotions.

> *"God, grant me the serenity to accept the things*
> *I cannot change, courage to change the things I*
> *can, and wisdom to know the difference."*
> —Reinhold Niebuhr

Disconnect and Clear to Connect

"Let's wander where the WiFi is
weakest to enjoy solitude."
—Kelle Sutliff

You need to put down those intrusive, addictive electronic devices. Spirit tells me this again and again. Spirit does not get Facebook, Instagram, Snap Chat, Twitter, and so forth. I wish they did. Can you imagine if they could all message us, just take a picture of themselves to say hello? Your loved ones would always be in touch. When you think about it, Spirit communicates like Instagram or Snap Chat. It is the same concept. Spirit gives us a picture, a glimpse of something, maybe an object or a phrase just when we need it, doesn't it? Spirit is its own social media platform.

You can connect to loved ones on the other side. If you ask them to give you a sign, please tell *them* the sign you're expecting. They will give it right back to you many times during the day. There is only one catch: To receive their messages, you have to be open to *flow*. Remember, you're all about the W (win). If you are always engaged on some screen, how can they connect to you and you to them? You can't.

Now, let's look at this realistically. One day you will be dead, right, and then you, too, will have to work within a loved one's aura of energy to get their attention so you can give them a message. Think how upset you would be if you constantly got that busy signal. "There she goes again, on Instagram. Look, another selfie. Now, she is texting. Now, she just clicked on Facebook to snoop. Ugh! I will never get ahold of her," your loved ones are saying on the other side. I would be really pissed if my kids or my husband did that to me. Where is a live person to talk to? Spirit waits and has to have a lot of patience.

You need to get off your technical devices and get into natural connection, to become a real human and not a tinfoil-hat person.

Connecting with *Flow* Exercise

It is your soul's job to center and create flow to receive communication. Here are some ideas.

Pick a space where you can feel comfortable—your favorite chair, the couch, your shower with that beautiful water flowing on you, or soaking in the bathtub. Wherever it is, *find it,* and make it your spot for being quiet every day.

Settle in and take a big, deep breath in and then blow it out. The oxygen in your breath fuels the cells in every inch of your physical form. Breathe in right down to your toes, and then exhale. Do this a couple of times. As you take hold of that breath, say kind words to yourself: **"I am healthy; I am whole." "I am free from (name it). "I am renewed." I am in God's energy for good."** The words can be your own. Speak in the present tense of the good that you deserve. Do not say you *hope* the good happens. Hope is too long term. You want specific results instantly, so be specific. "I want this instantly for my highest and best good and to benefit my family." Now, that kind of message will get the train up that mountain!

Take another breath and another. Each breath you take centers you into more quiet, and the quiet renews you, gives you the energy you had when you were born onto this earth. Your breath is creating the love that God gave you when you first came here. It is a hypnotic portal of calm and peace, and it is all you, 100 percent you. As you are breathing in and out deeply, close your eyes. When you are fully relaxed and your mind stops racing, you will find your peace.

Now, ask your questions. Your soul guidance is eager to give you your answers. Never doubt that. The first thoughts that come into your mind's eye are the answers. Breathe in and breathe out. Those answers and connections have been "on hold" for a long time, waiting for you. Say hello. *Namaste* is a simple greeting in Hindu. *Namaste*.

Now, it is time to call upon your loved ones, your guides, your God, your whole team, whoever they may be. You may feel alone, but you are not. Your team is in everything, remember? Your team's energy format is with you every step of the way—when you are born, as you live your life, and when you die. You need to get to know it. Psychic connection is your best friend.

Ask a question. The first thought that comes to you is your answer. The answer comes from your instinct. Answer equals instinct. Ask another question. The first thought that comes to you is your answer, from your instinct. Do it again. Ahhh, you have your answers. The psychic in you just linked to the other side, and wasn't that just amazing? You really are a natural at this. The more you practice, the more natural it will become.

You Are Grounded

As you get quiet to meditate, you are *grounding* your energy, which means you are grounded, literally. Not grounding and clearing your energy daily is like not taking a shower, and maybe not for years. Your energy feels like slick, oily sludge. Every emotion, every relationship, and every negative situation has stuck to your energy field. Someone, please pass the soap and washcloth. Let's get clean everyone. I am ready to teach you how.

Do you think it would be a good idea to clear your energy after a pandemic? For darn sure, and then some. Clearing your energy fields with meditation is refreshing, just like that fresh, clean smell on your body after you bathe. It is just as important as washing up. Carrying so much emotion and heaviness in your outer aura, which is your etheric energy, can leave weakness in your body. Remember, God put a lot of work into our physical, mental, and energy bodies. Our job is to maintain it. So, quit treating your aura like a pair of worn-out gym shoes you can't part with. It's time to head to the store for a new pair.

Of course, you can't go out and buy a new aura. It doesn't work like that. But what you *can* do is clear out the negative energy and keep it clear through a daily time of calm and receptivity. You will feel pretty good in that clean aura.

Now, as you sit breathing and relaxing, it's time to do the cleansing. Clearing your energy means realizing that you cannot control some situations. You need to free yourself of them and focus on what you *can* change. You have God, and you have your inner resources to overcome any difficult situation that you encounter, even if it feels desperate. Negativity will always try to sabotage you. It's time for you to switch it up.

In moments of difficulty, ask for guidance. Speak nicely to yourself. Affirm yourself. Say things like, **"Today, I am healthy. I am in the best shape. I am beautiful. I am peaceful. I am patient. I deserve kindness."** Use affirmations to compliment yourself. You are giving yourself this fantastic moment to refresh your cells, but *only* through peaceful breathing and kindness.

When you clear, you are renewing your faith in yourself, and this can be done in as little as two to five minutes. Mention anything that has disturbed you in your day, but then let it go. You can even be blunt and say, "I don't need this crap in my life, anymore." Just don't say, "*Truck* that!" That would be bad mediation!

As you end your energy clearing, affirm, **"For the highest and best good, I am cleared. Amen."**

How do you feel? I'll bet you're feeling clean, energized and ready to take your new sneakers out for a run.

Visualization

*"The positive thinker sees the invisible, feels
the intangible, and achieves the impossible."*
—Winston Churchill

The previous clearing exercises also protect your energy by shielding your aura to keep negativity from seeping in. Every day we clean our bodies, brush our teeth, wash our hair, provide our body with good food, and possibly even work out. At the same time, let's stop forgetting to protect our energy. We protect our homes. We don't just leave without locking it. It wouldn't make sense. I am saying that it's time to change. I know you have two minutes somewhere in the day to give your body a well-deserved healing.

Your Spirit body is magical. It is a veil of energy that is available to you all the time. It's like having a great neighbor. Neighbors look after one another's homes. They are kind to one another. Maybe all their kids play together, and maybe on a summer night, the adults meet up for a cocktail. You would not trade good neighbors for the world, right? They're like family. Well, your Spirit guidance and aura energy are just like good neighbors. They help you out.

Now that you are flowing in your energy and feeling so good, I want you to visualize that something really good is about to happen in your life. As an example, say you have a big sales account, and you need to close a deal for the end of the quarter. Envision it happening. See the signed contract and the date posted on it. Or, if you are having surgery, visualize your body part healed. If your child is trying to get into college, see her graduating from there.

It's not different from visualizing your child's upcoming football game. You visualize him making his tackle, holding the line, or catching the ball to make the touchdown. You don't see your child fumbling and fouling. You send good energy out onto the field. Now, do the same for yourself. Send out only good energy, because like always attract like. You always want to be on the positive end, not the negative one.

Visualization is powerful. We have all been born with the goods and the tools to use such methods, and I am here to remind you how to do it. The tools are part of your soul. If you are willing to quiet and calm yourself and embrace the benefits of connection, your life will change dramatically. Meditation time really is better than church, and you don't have to shake someone's hand during flu season! Your church is within you. God's energy is the peace within your soul. But if you are too loud all the time, you will not be able to hear it or experience its transformative effects.

Self Inc.—Growing Your Soul One Day at a Time

"Your mind, body and spirit are your best stock options. Create good investments."
—Kelle Sutliff

Look at the clearing exercises I have given with the view of a self-proprietor. You and God have the biggest and best company in the world. It's called Self Inc. The tagline on your business card is, "Growing my soul one day at a time." Wow, what a company! You and God are gonna knock it out of the park! You were always meant to be a respectful business partner to God, but you got lazy with your work. God is trusting you to hold up your end of the company. He's on the accounting and spreadsheet end, and you are in sales and promotions. If you slack on your end, no cash will come in for God to put in the spread sheet and this will reflect on your commission check.

How could you not do right by Self Inc.? The answer is on you. "Life got busy" is not the answer Spirit wants to hear. You forgot your hustle, plain and simple. You chose chaos over being centered in your energy, and that will always directly affect your end goal. You allowed yourself to get lazy and not care for the big three: your mind, body,

SPIRIT SPEAKS WITHIN YOU

and Spirit. God started you out with the perfect formula, and now it is time to get back to growing your soul with God's Spirit energy. Give Self Inc. a bright new future, back to the way it was intended to be. Make the money for God to put on your spreadsheet and you'll be able to pay the bills.

> *"Everything is energy and that is all there is to it. Match the frequency of the reality you want, and you cannot help but get that reality. It can be no other way. This is not philosophy. This is physics."*
> —Albert Einstein

Albert Einstein would approve of you getting back to work on your intuition. In my opinion, he was the most profound psychic of all time. He showed us the value of trusting our instincts.

The energy in the world today is giving our souls the opportunity to do things differently, to get back into the *flow* of trust and work towards that "W," that Win. Are you strengthening peaceful *flow* and trust? Sure you are, and you are quite deserving of the results, too. You have worked hard to create this opportunity for yourself. It really is quite amazing how one little shift, like taking time to be quiet, nourishes that rose, which is you, to grow out of the earth and bloom!

How to Communicate
with Spirit

*"We, as human beings, learn through
sharing and communicating."*
—Hugo Reynolds

"Ask and you shall receive." Remember, God told us that in the scriptures. As a little girl going to Catholic school and Mass twice a week, I thought, "I will just ask God for everything, and I will get it!" Soon, I realized I had to earn it before I could receive it. It's the same way for adults. We have to lay down the foundation for what we want, and then God's energy will push it our way—but always in divine time, when it is *supposed* to happen.

When you ask the Divine about your life's concerns, be sure to sit back and listen. The way people communicate with the Divine is all wrong. They just ask and ask and plead and plead. Kind of annoying, don't you think? Kind of like a three-year-old jumping up and down, crying, "Mama! Mama!" to get attention. Bluntly, the Divine may be pretty exhausted with you. It's time to shift. Stop being impatient. Instead of requesting your wishful outcome over and over, try shifting your efforts to getting the answers you need. Surprisingly, the answers may come from you.

Shocker! But you won't know unless you listen, listen, listen and act on what your guidance tells you. But no more behaving like a demanding three-year-old. Be patient.

My parents had a great saying for when life hit them hard with dynamics they couldn't change, like a stroke or a terminal cancer diagnosis: "It is what it is," which translates to acceptance, understanding, and working within the options you have. It also means you have to stay present and live in the present, not in the past. Do you know how hard that is to do when you are in despair? Everyone in the world felt this in 2020. We had to accept some outcomes we did not like and work through them.

Are you one of those people dwelling on your past? If so, I am telling you to *stop* that behavior instantly. Accept the "it is what it is" theory, and stay in the here and now, not ten years ago or even last year. Living in the past will just create chaos in your choices. It is time to think better and do better by yourself. Focus on Self Inc., and then you can start manifesting your integrity and love for yourself and others. Just be present. Our hardest times often lead to our greatest moments. Keep going.

> *"Rough situations build strong people in the end."*
> —Roy T. Bennett

Even when you meditate or pray to the Divine, you may not get your answer right away. You may get your answer through a sign or even from someone you speak with. The Divine speaks in many, many ways. If you are waiting for the Red Sea to part or Moses writing on his tablet to show you your answers, you will be waiting a while! And do you know that Spirit and God have a sense of humor? You will find it in messages. Oh, my gosh, the laughs they send us.

Here is one example. I was praying and asking for a sign to tell me which house to buy. I was sitting in mediation, thinking, "Okay, Spirit, lay it on me. My answer was a glazed donut! Moses wasn't there. Well, I went with it. I was visiting my tenth house of the day. As I drove down the street, I looked up to find a beige cement wheel with a hole in it that looked like a glazed donut, and on it was the street name! This marker was sitting on the corner lot that I would purchase. I laughed when I saw it and thought, "Okay, you got me!" We lived there for fourteen years. It was the house my kids grew up in. The land had a tranquil, centering feel to it, not to mention the good, homey energy with a little extra Spirit in it. And, of course, a glazed donut!

Another time while house hunting, I asked for a sign. Again, the jokesters were going to play me. This time I was given a green apple. What? Every home puts out a bowl of apples on the counter to make it "show worthy." I thought that sign was way too generic, but I went with it. After attending fifty showings, we walked into *the house*. My husband was in love with it. I was not taking the bait, yet. Where was my sign? There were no green apples on the counter. If I didn't see an apple anywhere, I was not buying that house. When I opened the laundry room cabinet, I saw a Green Apple Yankee Candle staring me down! I started to laugh. I thought, "Yep, you got me!"

I have given this psychic tip to many clients who are looking to purchase a home. The stories they come back with are on point! Remember, Spirit always has our back, even when it comes to our investments. You might want to step up your game and start letting it help you.

God and your passed loved ones leave signs all the time, trying to get your attention and give you answers. Most people in our society are too aloof from their intuition or too busy to listen. We've all been there. Sadly, we make hasty decisions without guidance, and when things don't turn out to our liking, we turn into frantic four-year-olds who can't get a cookie before dinner. Good things happen for those who are calm.

How do you ask for signs?

- Ask your question through prayer.
- Give God/Spirit your sign. It could be an object, a song, an animal, etc.
- Expect a response and give a timeline for an answer.
- Be patient and be observant.
- Be open to receive your answer/sign.
- Be thankful through prayer for being given the sign. Those on the other side use a lot of energy to send it to you.

Do this, and you will have just created the best internet out there, and it is just between you and God and *flow*. My twelve years of Catholic school did not teach me this connection. In second grade, with my hands folded on my desk, I really thought that if I said my prayers super hard, Moses was gonna show up! When it came to going to the board during math, we were told to pray a little harder and we would get our answers. They didn't teach us about the connection, and how to make the connection. Moses didn't come, and no answer came. What I did hear in my head was, "count on your fingers" and that's when I got the correct answer. I guess at age seven I already knew that I could trust my intuition.

It's time to get busy, ask your questions, and own your intuition. You can talk to Spirit through meditation. Heck, you don't even have to call it meditation. You can call it, "Going to the Ranch," "Sock-it-to-Me Moments," or "My Reveal." Make it just yours. By naming something, you create your boundaries, and you need boundaries when you meditate. I call my meditation time, "Kel's Korner." Intuitively, I claim my meditation space, and I always sit in a chair in the corner of the room. That's just what I do. As soon as you say the name of your quiet time/space, you begin to relax. I also use this name for a video series on my Kelle Sutliff YouTube channel.

Remember how carefully we considered what we should name our children and even our pets, wanting their names to hold meaning for us? Well, you are going to do the same thing for your daily time for yourself. And, don't include a negative term like *safe space*. Remember, you are already safe. God has seen to that.

The Divine will work with your breath and the quiet so that you can breathe in your good intentions and breathe out all your negativity. Shed all the ill will. Breathe in the good and exhale the unpleasant. It's not complicated. Just breathe in and breathe out. The divine energy always recognizes stable intentions. It won't forget about you. You are in a relationship with the Divine, and you have to do your part. You have to participate wholeheartedly to get the trophy, that is, to receive answers from your intuition.

The Divine is getting tired of all the takers. At some point, only the givers will be rewarded. It's quite fantastic to see the lessons that are being shown. In this unfolding future, no one will be able to walk between the raindrops. Spirit thinks it is about time to have accountability. Spirit is quite simple: you get what you give. I hope you are making good choices. Are you going to get the W for Win?

Remember the tagline for Self Inc. is: *Growing Your Soul One Day at a Time*. Be thankful for the team that is working with you: the Divine, your loved ones who have passed, your guides—all of them. Do you understand how much support you have? Talk about some magnificent mega management! There might be a saint, the Buddha, a monk or nun, or even an old girlfriend or boyfriend who has died. Passed loved ones never judge. You are safe. It is time to call in your team for guidance. *Source* is right there, giving you cues for confirmation. In the Catholic Mass, we say, "Peace be with you." I would like to change that to say, "Your team be with you." (Because they are.)

You are never ever alone. When you have tough times, you can learn to be humble and connect to your Three Wise Men. *Gather your good.* When I read for clients, Spirit points this out in every connection, especially when the client is going through difficult times. Some examples are a spouse dealing with bipolar activity and self-medicating who refuses to see a psychologist, the death of a loved one, or a child who is hurting. Those are punch-in-the-gut issues when you need your guides the most. It's part of human nature to feel lost. Then, we can strengthen our souls to reach our empowerment, which puts us into action mode.

I see Spirit kick into full gear, comforting my clients with messages and evidence. This powerful response proves to them and to me that we are *never* alone, even when dealing with a catastrophic illness. Our healing guides are even more powerful. They are praying for us. Yes, our guides pray for us.

My clients leave a reading feeling more comfortable. Spirit gives that to them in their messaging. I see it time and time again, even from a mother who has lost her two children to opiate overdoses or a mother who has lost her beloved only child to a motorcycle accident. The Divine in Spirit always comes through to teach us how to live again. Spirit understands how hard it is to live after someone you love dies. Our guides and our loved ones who have passed understand. They want to comfort and help your soul to heal, so let them. "Ask and you shall receive," remember?

The Universe communicates with you; it really does. You don't even need a medium to connect. Spirit gives you signs every day through your conversations, the radio, in your environment. Yes, Spirit even uses Facebook! Pay attention, note the patterns you see. Be aware.

Here is an example from Facebook: The other day, I was really missing my mom. In meditation that morning, I said, "Okay, Mom, I want you to show me yourself today. Two hours later, I opened Facebook. It was showing my Memories, and there was a photo of my mother in our gazebo, sitting on the couch with Moe, one of our corgis!

I laughed with tears in my eyes. "Thank you!" The photo was just what I needed to comfort me in my grief. You see, that is an example of Spirit on a mission. Our guides are available to us. All we have to do is ask.

We held hands with our children as we crossed the street when they were small, telling them to stay close. We kept watch on the surroundings as we waited for the light to change from red to green. We were more aware of the environment to keep our kids safe, our instinct in full-throttle mode.

Spirit works in the same way, always aware, always protecting you from harm. Your angels and guides try hard to help you, but sometimes you jump out into the street without looking or thinking of the consequences, and boom! You get hit! Spirit wants to work with you to prevent these accidents so you can be at ease and stay safe. It is up to you to provide that kind of aid to your Self Inc. Remember your motto: ***"Growing Your Soul One Day at a Time"*** and hold on tight. Spirit never lets you go.

You don't need any more clutter or chaos. Our world is so much louder than it was even twenty years ago. Loud used to be a concert that left our ears ringing for days. We took more time with life. Today, if things are not done in a nanosecond, we freak out! Think of the crazy pressure we put on our vital energy, not to mention our physical bodies. We are destroying Self Inc. We need to step back and take time to listen to Spirit within.

Wrong Net

"Closing the door to toxicity is the most effective way to make space for new opportunity."
—Amy Chan

The Internet is a great communication tool, one of the best inventions ever. It transformed us, just like Ford's mass production of the car or Tesla's discovery of the electrical current. We cannot live without them, right? Wonderful as it is, Spirit doesn't want us to get so caught up in it that all we do is surf the net. But sadly, we are addicted to the Internet and apps are making our energetic field robotic and keeping us out of karmic *flow*.

We need to be conscious of maintaining an acceptable interface with the technology we are allowing to enter the wholeness of our bodies. This interference is caustic to your own special body. You don't drive your car around in circles every day just because you can. When you get a vaccine, you don't say, "Doc, give me another just for good measure." You don't keep flicking the light switch on and off just because you need to see your electricity work. So, why do we immerse ourselves in this technology twenty-four/seven? Too much of this frequency is harming you.

What are you are missing in your life that you feel the need to tell the world your story? Everyone is an actor today, and, sadly, without the pay. We are allowing our fake selves to control our etheric energy, not our authentic selves. What does Spirit advise? Stop posting so much, stop displaying your intimate details on the Internet because, guess what? Frankly, Internet apps are not your best friend. Does anyone really care that you have a date tonight or that you're eating fish? Now, if you could turn one fish into hundreds, like Jesus did, that would make a phenomenal post! Now, that's a post I would *like*.

How about liking yourself a little more instead of clicking hearts or thumbs up? Spirit wants you to throw yourself some of those hearts and thumbs up your own way. You deserve emojis, too. Spirit within you is starving. Spirit wants you to like yourself instead of preoccupying yourself with social media. You are forgetting you and obsessing on something that is irrelevant.

I am a woman who loves a power outage here and there and vacations with bad cell service. A good rainy day is my jam. Spirit wants you off your grid so you can relax and get centered, like in the good old days. It is time to find some peace.

As I write this, I am in the Bahamas on a beach. I hear the waves lapping on the sand. The wind is blowing, and the sun is warm on my body. My phone is off, but I can hear the dings—I counted six of them. I know I can get to them later. I'm not letting the phone ruin my moment. I am taking it *all* in: it's just me, Spirit, a long beach, and a cocktail at my side.

When you are in the moment, don't let anything ruin it. There are some great moments in which manifestation can occur when your clear space makes you powerful. If you continue on that path, your rewards will be deep in value.

Children's Connection
to Nature

*"Nature's beauty is a gift that cultivates
appreciation and gratitude."*
—Louie Schwartzberg

Wow, has the internet changed our children's etheric life force—and *dramatically!* Parents, you are killing your children's auras with all these electronic devices. The only "net" our kids should be playing with is a soccer, tennis, or basketball net. Parents, let your kids feel the outdoors. Nature is the best teacher. Some famous people understood this quite well:

"Nature always wears the colors of the Spirit."
—Ralph Waldo Emerson

*"If you truly love nature, you will
find beauty everywhere."*
—Laura Ingalls Wilder

You own your children's energy until they move out of the house and start paying their first mortgage. That's a long time. You need to protect their energy to keep them grounded. It's okay to say *no* to your kids, to teach them boundaries and good rewards. It's okay for parents to make sure their kids smell like a sweaty summer shirt. That's how you know your kids have had a good day. Get those kids outside, let them play, let them organize their own games with their friends, let them sit on the lawn talking about girls or boys "they like." Let your kids climb trees or hop fences or do a "runny" off into the water. Let them breathe in life.

> *"Be the energy you want others to absorb."*
> —A. D. Posey

My children sure did experience these adventures, and both my husband and I had that advantage, also. Let your kids build forts in the woods, fish, and explore. Get them outside. Get them involved in team sports. But, dear Lord, please get them off their devices so that they can connect with the best source of all for their intuitive vibration, Mother Earth.

> *"On earth there is no heaven, but*
> *there are pieces of it."*
> —Jules Renard

Spirit wants your children to feel the earth and let the earth teach them. Nature never fails us. It connects psychically with our children and feeds them the grace of nature. Nature will always be our best teacher. Remember, we are all flowers that can bloom into something amazing.

Our kids need nature, so don't screw them up with device addiction.

"Nature is the art of God."
—Dante Alighieri

God has provided a beautiful palette, so why not let your kids out to enjoy it? I wish you could see what I see. I can see their auras bouncing above them when they play outside. Maybe you don't have to see what I see. Just take my word for it.

Feeling nature will make your children more grounded. It is pretty simple, and everyone needs simple after a pandemic. Does your family take walks together? Do you have a fire pit outside under the stars? Heck, did you pitch a tent in the backyard? Or did you have a conference call during the pandemic and throw them on their tablets for three hours? Knowing what you know now, you can always change your parenting style. Maybe what we have learned will be fantastic for the whole family. Part of keeping our children whole is to encourage them to live without tattered holes in their energy field.

Parenting has been hard in 2020/2021, but for their energy's sake, I hope you tried to fill it with activities outdoors. Have you tried this great new app called Old School Parenting? It sends the kids out to play after school. You tell them, "See you at five p.m. for dinner. You have two full hours to play outside. You can even play more after you eat dinner. When the streetlights come on, though, you had better be home! My generation and those before were blessed to play hard outside and get dirty. Our kids need this natural connection to Spirit.

Loss and Grief

Our loved ones never really leave us. They can't get rid of us that easy! We are connected by a love vibration, even if we hated each other here on this earth. Heaven gives us hope to work through disharmony, because love lives on forever. If you have lost someone in this ugly pandemic, whatever the cause, keep Spirit in your back pocket. Your loved ones connect to you in many ways: nature, funny symbols, words, visions. You name it, and they will send it to you.

I deal with grieving people every day in my work. I understand what death does to people, but I also know the hope and endless caring your lost loved ones give back to you. They will never forget you. They just won't. Death is a mind-set. You can either look at it as the ending or the beginning.

Spirit has shown me that death is all about beginnings, a type of renewal that we, too, will experience one day. Your loved ones have a strong vibration through which they can bridge memories back and forth to you easily.

They connect to Spirit within you. Be receptive to the connection and watch how the two of you continue to bloom.

I want to share a poem I received from Michele Bourgeois whose son I helped recover in Littleton, CO through a reading during a psychic investigation. For three weeks she had no leads on the disappearance of her son until we worked together. Graham was found in the water location I gave her along with his boot as a marker for evidence. I told her he would be found only a few miles from his residence and that his death would be an accident. I also gave her three family members names whom Graham was with, in Spirit, confirming that I knew he had passed. Tragically, Graham died from falling through an iced-over lake.

Michele found this poem after Graham had passed, and she shared it with me. I can tell you that he was listening to the Divine when he wrote these heartfelt words:

"I'm lost and gone, but I am here now. Where are you, have we crossed the same ground? Think of me and I will think of you. Together we'll be in a place we once knew. Could it be that we're here simultaneously? Oh, the irony, but I shall walk free... God does not grant power to those who are closer to him. What God really grants you is the ability to be powerless in the mercy of him."
—Graham Michael Hebert

Affirmations for Communicating with Spirit

We all know how important powerful intentions can be. They are part of how we manifest and implement "the good" in our future. Intentions help us clear negative situations so that we don't carry that negativity with us during this lifetime. Remember, your connection to this guidance is your best friend. It communicates with you, heals, and protects you so that you feel settled and complete. But only when you ask can you receive.

When Spirit Speaks within you, be prepared to listen and to act. Using affirmations is one of the best ways to achieve your goals. Try the affirmations below, but also feel free to create your own affirmations in the way that you and your inner connections know best.

- When I face fears in my life, I no longer accept weak behavior. I am strong, I am strength ... and so it is.
- My new vocabulary is *flow*. I am accomplished in my goals ... and so it is.
- I accept divine order in my life. I will be patient with the outcomes, and when I receive these outcomes, I will be thankful ... and so it is.

- I acknowledge that hate is an emotion, but I refuse to let hate define my soul ... and so it is.
- If I felt worthless during a tragedy in my life, I accept the lesson, but the tragedy does not define me. Only I can define me. I am resilient ... and so it is.
- I am healthy, and I am whole ... and so it is. (This is a good one to repeat daily when you are experiencing mental or physical challenges.)
- I am protected by spiritual light from God every day ... and so it is.
- My children are good citizens and have happiness, love, and accomplishment in their lives ... and so it is.
- My freedoms are sovereign and are protected so that I can provide for myself, my family, and the good of mankind ... and so it is.
- We are free within society of oppressive restrictions and our world has freedom for our highest and best good ... and so it is.
- I am no longer selfish. I see the needs of others so that I can be a really good human ... and so it is.
- I am thankful now for all the abundance that will fill my life ... and so it is.
- As hard as it is to accept change, I have accepted it. Now, I prosper within all of this new opportunity ... and so it is.
- My intuitive leadership is on fire ... and so it is.

- I do not blame anyone for my choices. I have overcome being a victim ... and so it is.
- I am one heck of a business executive. I am recognized for my accomplishments at work ... and so it is.
- I am protected by my ancestors and my guides everywhere I go. I am so thankful for their protection ... and so it is.
- My land, my home, and my country are protected always from evil ... and so it is.
- I am protected from false information, and I have the courage and integrity to know the difference ... and so it is.
- I am relaxed. I am no longer kinetic, and so I can receive answers to my questions from Spirit ... and so it is.
- I give a sign to a passed loved one today, and I am aware now to receive it ... and so it is.
- I am listening to my psychic instinct as it guides me into perfect decision-making ... and so it is.
- I am no longer a dandelion. I am a rose blooming in life's natural synchronicity ... and so it is.
- The Patriots, The Red Sox, and The Bruins win every championship ... and so it is! (This one is very important! ☺)

Affirmations to Share with Your Children

- I have passed my test today, and I deserve a good grade ... and so it is.
- I have awesome, honorable friendships ... and so it is.
- I am grounded like the root of a tree ... and so it is.
- I have gotten into my best trade school or college so that I can create the best career ... and so it is.
- I pick respectful, kind partners to share my love with ... and so it is.

Your Last Message:
Channeled by Kelle

You are now grown up! You are that Spirit within you. Many tools have been shared. You are alive with knowledge, but be aware of false knowledge, for ignorance can be dangerous. You are one amazing soul.

See yourself as a soul, and you will see others as the same. You are no different. I am no different. Your essence as that soul is love. Honoring yourself and your brethren will bring you abundance. Your soul will dance to the heartbeat of humanity, and isn't that amazing?

God's energy protects and heals, but you can't have it or hear it if you are too complicated. Uncomplicate yourself, and Spirit within will grow us together. Just like a flower piercing through my earth, we will bloom once again. If you pray with pure heart and intuition, I will hear you and respond. *"Follow your soul and Spirit within you. It always knows the way."*

I honor that place in you in which the entire universe dwells. I honor the place in you which is love, light, peace, and joy. When you are in that place inside you, and I am in that place in Me. We are one. Namaste.

You are one beautiful soul, enjoying all-new vibrancy, and so it will be ... from me to you.
—Kelle

About the Author

Kelle Sutliff is an Internationally renowned psychic medium, psychic investigator and speaker who has appeared on national and international television and radio programs.

Her first book, ***Listen Up! The Other Side IS Talking***, has won the internationally acclaimed **Reader's Favorite** and **Mom's Choice** book awards.

Kelle has demonstrated that the psychic world is very real for more than 18 years. Her gifts and insights have provided inspiration and comfort to many people dealing with grief and loss. She is also a sought-after psychic investigator, working with families and private investigators on current and cold cases.

Kelle is known for her accurate predictions on world events and within her clients' lives. Her national and international clients include celebrities, professionals, and business executives.

For more information about Psychic Medium Kelle and to book a reading, please visit
PsychicMediumKelle.com

Praise for Psychic Medium Kelle Sutliff

"Kelle is a true gift to people in their lives... She has an incredible gift from Spirit, and her accuracy is second to none ... Kelle's readings are completely honest and compassionate. She has amazed me with her accuracy ... a truly blessed medium."
—Emilia Kelly, International Clairvoyant Consultant, Buckinghamshire, UK

"Parapsychology as a field has been largely dismissed as not scientific. And nothing could be farther from the truth. Life is a fascinating experience that can be reduced down to the activities of organic matter bound by space and time. We are so much more than just chemical processes. All that being said, Kelle is a friend and confidante who is incredibly talented in connecting to the mysteries of our lives beyond the now."
—Lawrence Peacock, MD

"Not long after my son had passed, I had the opportunity to work with Kelle. She gave me an impromptu reading, connecting me to my son. I was shocked at her accuracy. She knew things that she had no way of knowing. I was so grateful to hear my son's messages and know they were absolutely authentic. Kelle Sutliff is the 'Real Deal.'"

—Leora Leon, TV Host, *"The Power in You,"* Divine Path Life Coach and Energy Healer

Also Available from
Kelle Sutliff

Listen Up! The Other Side IS Talking

Winner of the international prestigious Mom's Choice Award and the Readers' Favorite Award!

In this book, Kelle shares her psychic medium experiences in an honest and straightforward manner. You will better understand how mediums do the work they do and how you, the reader, can also benefit from "waking up" to your own abilities. It is with humor and grace that Kelle walks us through the process of learning to trust our inner knowing. Her message is very clear; we all need to pay attention to the signs and symbols that passed loved ones give us every day as they want to comfort us in our time of grief. This book explains how this communication works and how to listen.

"Kelle Sutliff is a wonderful evidential medium and radio personality. Her book (Listen Up! The Other Side IS Talking) is enlightening, entertaining and will open you up to the reality of spirit contact."
—Mark Anthony, The Psychic Lawyer®

For more information, please visit
psychicmediumkelle.com/books

Additional Materials and Resources

Access your Additional Materials & Resources here
PsychicMediumKelle.com/sswybonus